MILLER ELEMENTARY SCHOOL
130 E. JACKSON
CEMENT CITY, MICHIGAN 49233

THE IMPORTANCE OF

Jim Thorpe

These and other titles are included in The Importance Of
biography series:

Alexander the Great

Napoleon Bonaparte

Cleopatra

Christopher Columbus

Marie Curie

Thomas Edison

Albert Einstein

Benjamin Franklin

Galileo Galilei

Jim Henson

Thomas Jefferson

Chief Joseph

Malcolm X

Margaret Mead

Michelangelo

Wolfgang Amadeus Mozart

Sir Isaac Newton

Richard M. Nixon

Jackie Robinson

Anwar Sadat

Margaret Sanger

John Steinbeck

Jim Thorpe

Mark Twain

H.G. Wells

Jim Thorpe

by
Don Nardo

Lucent Books, P.O. Box 289011, San Diego, CA 92198-9011

Library of Congress Cataloging-in-Publication Data

Nardo, Don, 1947-
    Jim Thorpe / by Don Nardo
        p. cm.—(The Importance of)
    Includes bibliographical references and index.
    ISBN 1-56006-045-X
    1. Thorpe, Jim, 1888-1953—Juvenile literature. 2. Athletes—
United States—Biography—Juvenile literature. 3. Indians of
North America—Biography—Juvenile literature. I. Series.
GV697.T5N37   1994
796'.092—dc20   93-41138
[B]   CIP
                                                                  AC

Copyright 1994 by Lucent Books, Inc., P.O. Box 289011,
San Diego, California, 92198-9011

Printed in the U.S.A.

Contents

Foreword

THE IMPORTANCE OF biography series deals with individuals who have made a unique contribution to history. The editors of the series have deliberately chosen to cast a wide net and include people from all fields of endeavor. Individuals from politics, music, art, literature, philosophy, science, sports, and religion are all represented. In addition, the editors did not restrict the series to individuals whose accomplishments have helped change the course of history. Of necessity, this criterion would have eliminated many whose contribution was great, though limited. Charles Darwin, for example, was responsible for radically altering the scientific view of the natural history of the world. His achievements continue to impact the study of science today. Others, such as Chief Joseph of the Nez Percé, played a pivotal role in the history of their own people. While Joseph's influence does not extend much beyond the Nez Percé, his nonviolent resistance to white expansion and his continuing role in protecting his tribe and his homeland remain an inspiration to all.

These biographies are more than factual chronicles. Each volume attempts to emphasize an individual's contributions both in his or her own time and for posterity. For example, the voyages of Christopher Columbus opened the way to European colonization of the New World. Unquestionably, his encounter with the New World brought monumental changes to both Europe and the Americas in his day. Today, however, the broader impact of Columbus's voyages is being critically scrutinized. *Christopher Columbus,* as well as every biography in The Importance Of series, includes and evaluates the most recent scholarship available on each subject.

Each author includes a wide variety of primary and secondary source quotations to document and substantiate his or her work. All quotes are footnoted to show readers exactly how and where biographers derive their information, as well as to provide stepping stones to further research. These quotations enliven the text by giving readers eyewitness views of the life and times of each individual covered in The Importance Of series.

Finally, each volume is enhanced by photographs, bibliographies, chronologies, and comprehensive indexes. For both the casual reader and the student engaged in research, The Importance Of biographies will be a fascinating adventure into the lives of people who have helped shape humanity's past and present, and who will continue to shape its future.

Important Dates in the Life of Jim Thorpe

Sac and Fox Indians defeated by the United States Army in the Black Hawk War.	**1831-1832**
Jim Thorpe born on May 28 near Bellemont, Oklahoma.	**1880** — Hiram P. Thorpe, Jim's father, moves to Oklahoma.
	1888
Twin brother Charlie dies of pneumonia.	**1893** — Attends first school in Stroud, Oklahoma.
	1896
Glenn "Pop" Warner begins coaching at Carlisle Indian School in Pennsylvania.	**1898** — Begins attending Haskell Institute in Lawrence, Kansas.
	1899
Meets Pop Warner and makes the varsity track and football teams.	**1904** — Jim Thorpe arrives at Carlisle; father dies of blood poisoning.
	1907
Wins many games and medals, establishing himself as one of the best athletes in the nation.	**1908** — Wins many games and medals, establishing himself as one of the best athletes in the nation.
	1909
	1912
Wins Decathlon and Pentathlon at 1912 Olympics; hailed as greatest athlete in the world.	**1913** — Plays minor-league baseball in summer for money.
	1915
	1917 — Loses Olympic medals and trophies for playing baseball for money.
Begins playing professional football; son James Jr. born.	**1920** — Son dies.
Becomes president of the American Professional Football Association.	**1929**
Begins lecture tour on sports and Indian issues.	**1937** — Plays last professional football game.
	1945 — Joins U.S. Merchant Marine.
Named greatest football player of first half of twentieth century; also named greatest all-around male athlete of same period.	**1950**
	1951 — Hollywood film *Jim Thorpe—All American* released.
	1953
Dies on March 28 in Lomita, California.	**1954** — National Football League introduces Most Valuable Player trophy, naming it after Jim Thorpe.
	1958
Posthumously elected to the National Indian Hall of Fame.	**1983** — Olympic medals posthumously restored.

The Concept of an American Indian Hero

i hate this class

Jim Thorpe has been almost universally acknowledged as the world's greatest athlete during the first half of the twentieth century. His exploits in football and track and field are legendary. Among other formidable feats, he could kick a field goal from the fifty-yard line and high jump over six feet with equal ease and agility. And his performance at the 1912 Olympic Games in Sweden remains nothing less than spectacular. Competing in both the Decathlon and Pentathlon, a total of fifteen grueling events, he won both contests and received worldwide acclaim.

But the importance of Thorpe's achievements, great as they were, extends beyond the playing fields and record books. As a Sac and Fox Indian, he was part of a bigger sports phenomenon of the early decades of the century that has since been largely forgotten. This was the ascendancy of Native American athletes as national sports heroes. Thorpe was the most famous member of a number of excellent and often invincible football teams fielded by Carlisle Indian School in Pennsylvania in the years immediately preceding World War I. Led by Glenn "Pop" Warner, one of the greatest coaches in the history of the game, Carlisle regularly defeated the best schools in the country. Thorpe and his teammates thrilled the nation as they outran and outplayed such gridiron giants as Harvard, Syracuse, and West Point. And the Native American teams pioneered many of the formations and plays that later became standard in the sport. *bullshit*

Jim Thorpe demonstrates his kicking skill in a 1912 Carlisle vs. Toronto game.

At the time, most white Americans were surprised and amazed by the Carlisle school's victories. When Thorpe entered Carlisle in 1904, barely fourteen years had passed since the massacre of 153 American Indians by the United States Army at Wounded Knee, South Dakota. This was the final violent episode in the long battle

Thorpe as a Carlisle player in 1912.

between whites and Native Americans for possession of North America. By the mid-1890s, most of the 250,000 Indians in the United States lived in poverty on reservations designated by the government. The majority of whites believed that the defeat and subjugation of Native Americans was inevitable because whites were superior, and thus many people were used to viewing the whites as heroes and the Indians as villains. These people were unprepared for the concept of an American Indian hero and found the athletic superiority of Thorpe and his teammates both inexplicable and astounding.

For the Carlisle players, victory over the whites on the playing field was a matter of pride, not only for their school, but for their race as well. At the time, athletics was the one arena in which Native Americans could compete equally with whites. And Thorpe and his colleagues took full advantage of the opportunity. Pop Warner later recalled:

> Carlisle had no traditions, but what the Indians did have was a real race pride and a fierce determination to show the palefaces what they could do when the odds were even. It was not that they felt any definite bitterness against the conquering white or against the government for years of unfair treatment, but rather that they believed the armed contests between red man and white had never been waged on equal terms.[1]

In time, Carlisle's glory faded. The school sank from the national spotlight, and over the years new generations of football fans grew up unaware of Native Americans' contributions to the sport. Today, few people remember great Indian

Some of the Native Americans Thorpe led in a 1932 protest of Hollywood's casting of non-Indians in Indian roles.

athletes like Gus Welch and Albert Exendine, who helped drive Carlisle to its many victories. But the name Jim Thorpe lives on. Part of his great legacy is a fabulous athletic career filled with thrilling and amazing accomplishments. Yet he also remains a symbol of a forgotten era, a reminder to the world that once, in the only contests in which whites and American Indians met as equals, the Indians won.

1 The Outdoorsman

Jim Thorpe and his twin brother Charlie were born on May 28, 1888, in a log cabin a few miles south of the small Oklahoma town of Bellemont. Their parents were poor farmers. Charlotte Viewx, their mother, was a member of the Potawatomi Indian tribe, a people originally known for their skills in crafts and fire-making tools. The boys' father, Hiram Thorpe, known in the area as "Big Hiram" because of his imposing size, was half Sac and Fox Indian and half Irish.

Following the tradition of many Native Americans, Charlotte gave her new sons Indian as well as Christian names. It was a Sac and Fox tribal custom for the mother to name a child after a memorable experience from her pregnancy or from the moments directly following birth. Jim had come into the world shortly after sunrise. At that moment, Charlotte had glanced out the window and seen the front path bathed in the glow of the rising sun. So she named him Wa-Tho-Huck, meaning "Bright Path." Charlotte and Hiram did not know at the time that this choice of name was prophetic. They did not dream of just how bright a path Jim would follow,

Members of the Sac and Fox tribe on the American plains in the early 1800s.

A typical Sac and Fox bark house in 1875.

one day becoming a world-famous athlete and the most renowned Native American of the twentieth century.

The Sac and Fox Migrations

Young Jim's name was only a small part of the Native American heritage he received from his parents. From the time he could walk and talk, he learned about the deeds of his Sac and Fox ancestors and about how his family had made its way to Oklahoma. This knowledge of his heritage gave him a sense of pride and through the years helped him cope with the difficulties of growing up as an Indian in a white-dominated land. Charlotte and Hiram told Jim and their other children how the Sac and the Fox were once two separate tribes living in southern Canada and on the shores of the Great Lakes. The Sac, the "people of the yellow earth," and the Fox, the "people of the red earth," lived in large, bark-covered cottages and grew crops such as corn and beans. They also

hunted buffalo for meat and for hides to make clothes. In the early 1700s, facing threats by French colonists and other Indian tribes, the Sac and Fox peoples joined forces. Many of the Sac and Fox subsequently migrated into what are now the states of Illinois, Wisconsin, and Missouri, but they did not escape the ravages of war. In the late 1700s, they fought many battles against the Osage and Cherokee tribes.

Eventually, the Sac and Fox faced a more formidable challenge—the relentless westward movement of white American settlers. Some members of the tribe wanted to sell large tracts of their land to the whites. But others, like Chief Black Hawk, Jim Thorpe's great-great-grandfather, advocated resistance to white demands. In his autobiography, Black Hawk later wrote:

> My reason teaches me that the land cannot be sold. The Great Spirit gave it to his children to live upon, and cultivate; as far as is necessary for their subsistence, they have the right to the soil. . . . Nothing can be sold, but such things as can be carried away.[2]

From 1831 to 1832, Black Hawk rallied his warriors against the whites in what became known as the Black Hawk War. But the United States Army defeated the Sac and Fox and threw Black Hawk into prison.

After its defeat, the tribe moved into Iowa, and later into Kansas and Oklahoma. It was during these years of constant migration that an Irish trapper named Hiram G. Thorpe met and married No-ten-o-quah, a member of Black Hawk's clan. Their son, Hiram P. Thorpe, though half Irish, had no recognizable white features. In fact, tribal elders often remarked on how much the boy resembled his ancestor, Black Hawk. Apparently, Hiram P. also inherited from Black Hawk

(Above) Black Hawk, the great Sac and Fox chief. (Below) Jim Thorpe's grandparents: Hiram G. Thorpe (left) and No-ten-o-quah.

the gift of physical prowess. Black Hawk had been renowned for his feats of strength and endurance, and as young Hiram grew up, he too became the tribe's greatest athlete. As biographer Gregory Richards put it, Hiram became:

> a strapping muscular man, standing more than six feet tall and weighing well over two hundred pounds. Like his Indian forefathers, Hiram loved physical challenges. He became known among the Sac and Fox as the best wrestler, swimmer, and rider for miles around. He was the undisputed champion of almost any sports contest.[3]

Later, Hiram passed on his love for athletics and the outdoors to his son Jim, who would eventually carry the family's history of physical achievement to new heights.

Working and Playing Hard

In 1880 Hiram moved with other members of the tribe to the Sac and Fox reservation in Oklahoma, where he received a 160-acre tract of land from the U.S. government. There, he married on three separate occasions, the third time to Charlotte Viewx, who eventually bore him

A True Indian

After being captured by the U.S. Army in 1832, Chief Black Hawk made a farewell speech to his people. His words, quoted by Jack Newcombe in The Best of the Athletic Boys, *warned that Indians might someday become too much like the whites. Ironically, his famous descendant, Jim Thorpe, would gain success by becoming accepted in the white world.*

"An Indian who is as bad as a white man could not live in our nation; he would be put to death and eaten by the wolves. The white men are bad schoolmasters; they carry false looks and deal in false actions; they smile in the face of the poor Indian to cheat him; they shake him by the hand to gain his confidence, to make him drunk, to deceive him, to ruin his wife. . . . We are not safe. We live in danger. We are becoming like them; hypocrites and liars, adulterers, lazy drones; all talkers and no workers. . . . Black Hawk is a true Indian, and disdains to cry like a woman. He feels for his wife, his children, and his friends. But he does not care for himself. He cares for his nation, and the Indians. They will suffer. He laments their fate. The white men do not scalp the head; but they do worse—they poison the heart; it is not pure with them. His countrymen will not be scalped, but they will, in a few years, become like the white man, so that you cannot trust them."

the twins—Jim and Charlie. At the time they were born, Hiram already had a son, Frank, and a daughter, Minnie, from a previous marriage, as well as George, a son by Charlotte. Later, Charlotte had several other children, although some of them died in childhood. High rates of infant mortality were not unusual among Indian farm families in the area. Living conditions were difficult at best. The winters were harsh; houses lacked electricity, running water, or sewage facilities; and doctors were scarce. Thus, usually only the strongest children survived.

Because their father was a farmer, Jim Thorpe and his siblings grew up mainly in the outdoors and learned about raising both crops and animals. Remembering

Thorpe posed for this formal portrait in 1907 when he was nineteen.

the farm and the hard work it took to maintain it, Jim's boyhood friend Art Wakolee later wrote:

> Like the other Sac and Fox, [Hiram] planted a wide variety of crops and raised a modest number of horses, cattle, hogs, and chickens. He always raised enough to live on during the winter: dried corn, pumpkins, beans, fruits, and meat, both wild and tame. Actually, Charlotte, following Indian custom, planted and worked the field. After the men had cleared the fields by burning, the women would take over and break up the earth with digging sticks or hoes made from shells or bones. The women had to keep the crows from the corn and also harvested it. Besides their field work, the women cared for the children, made clothing, wove, and cooked. After clearing the land for farming, the men made tools and weapons, hunted, and organized the religious and political functions [of the community].[4]

Young Jim was expected to do his share of the demanding chores on the farm. In addition to helping his mother in the fields, he fed the livestock and learned to rope horses. Yet the boy did not spend all his time working. Hiram's love of athletics, games, and physical activities of all kinds was infectious, and Jim learned early to play as hard as he worked. "Our lives were lived in the open, winter and summer," Jim later recalled. "We were never in the house when we could be out of it. And we played hard. I emphasize this because the boys who would grow up strong men must lay the foundations in a vigorous youth."[5]

The most lasting and memorable gift Hiram gave Jim was a skill and love for

Lives Lived in the Open

"Up to the time that little Charlie died at the age of eight of pneumonia, we roamed the prairies and swam and played together always. After Charlie's death, I used to go out by myself with an old dog and hunt coon when I was only nine years old. Often I would make camp and stay out all night. Later, my older brother, George, became my playmate and to equal him in our games I had to be strong and active. As I grew older I had other playmates in the young Indians from the neighboring reservations. As I look back at them, they were a husky crowd. Our lives were lived in the open, winter and summer. We were never in the house when we could be out of it. And we played hard. I emphasize this because the boys who would grow up strong men must lay the foundation in a vigorous youth. Our favorite game was 'Follow the Leader.' Depending on the 'leader,' that can be made an exciting game. Many a time in following I had to swim rivers, climb trees, and run under horses. But our favorite was climbing hickory or tall cedar trees, getting on the top, swinging there and leaping to the ground, ready for the next 'follow.' I swam a great deal. Indeed, I lived in the water. It is great exercise. For the development of muscle and wind I cannot recommend it too highly."

hunting. "In addition to playing the games of childhood," Jim wrote:

I spent a great deal of my time in hunting and fishing. I was always of a restless disposition and never was content unless I was trying my skill in some game against my fellow playmates or testing my endurance and wits against some member of the animal kingdom, of which there were many in that part of Oklahoma where I spent my youthful days. I became well versed in forest lore. I particularly loved to hunt and fish. I learned how to wait beside a runway [animal path] and stalk a deer. I learned how to trap for bear and rabbits, coon, and possum.[6]

Jim's eagerness and natural hunting ability helped forge a strong bond between father and son. In addition, Hiram soon realized that there was something special about the boy. Of all the Thorpe children, Jim seemed to be the only one to have inherited his father's amazing physical energy and endurance. Jim later remembered:

> I have never known a man with so much energy as my father. He could walk, ride, or run for days without ever showing the least sign of fatigue. Once, when we didn't have enough horses to carry all our kill [from a hunt] my father slung a buck deer over each shoulder and carried them twenty miles to our home.[7]

The Reservation School

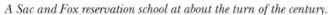

Although Hiram believed that teaching his sons about hunting, fishing, and games was important, he did not think skills in these areas were enough to prepare the boys for manhood. In a white-dominated world in which Indians were seen as second-class citizens, only the most educated Indians had even the slightest chance for success. Hiram and Charlotte agreed that their children should get the best education possible. So in 1893, when they were six years old, Jim and Charlie began attending and boarding at the reservation school in Stroud, about twenty-five miles from the farm.

From the beginning, young Jim disliked school. This was partly because he was unhappy about being away from home. In any event, at the time, his school, like many other reservation schools around the country, was substandard in comparison to the average white American school. For one thing, the white teachers at the reservation schools often lacked proper training. To get certified,

A Sac and Fox reservation school at about the turn of the century.

they had only to pass a government test of minimal difficulty. Also, there were often too few books to go around and these books were in English, which was still a strange language to most Indian children. Art Wakolee remembered:

> We could not speak or understand English when we were taken there at the age of six. It took us a long time to learn our lessons in kindergarten because most of the teachers had very little patience with the Indian children. Some of the teachers were kind, while others were very mean. We got a licking many times when we could not spell a simple word. As a result, we could not learn very much because most of us were afraid of our teacher.[8]

Three things helped Jim Thorpe cope with his unhappiness at the reservation school. First, he had the constant companionship of his twin brother Charlie, with whom he was very close. Second, Jim's older brother George often lectured him on the importance of school, telling him that he must try to become as literate and wise as his famous ancestor, Black Hawk. The third thing that made Jim's school days bearable was his discovery of baseball and other sports. He later wrote:

> My first experience with baseball was at the Agency School. George gave me my first lessons and soon I was playing every afternoon. We called it prairie baseball. Teams would be chosen and the game would be played out in the field. That is the equivalent of what is called sand-lot baseball today. We were also interested in basketball, but we had no track because it was a day when track was a passé [outdated] idea.

Thorpe at Carlisle Indian School in 1908.

Only the Indians participated in this type of activity and it was of an unofficial nature, the only regularly scheduled event being the weekly meet in front of my father's house.[9]

What little fun Jim found in the reservation school was quickly forgotten late in 1896 when he was eight. His brother Charlie contracted pneumonia. Family and friends did what they could, but there were no well-trained doctors in the region and Charlie died. Though grief-stricken,

Haskell Institute, an all Indian school in Lawrence, Kansas, as it appeared in the early 1900s.

young Jim followed the tradition of many Native American tribes whereby men and boys refused to show their feelings outwardly. As would be the case with the tragedies he faced throughout his life, he mourned his twin solemnly and quietly.

With Charlie gone, Jim felt he could no longer bear to attend the reservation school and informed his parents that he wanted to stay home and help with the farm. But Hiram sternly insisted that the boy return to school. The elder Thorpe told his son that without an education he would have little chance of having a productive life. Reluctantly, Jim obeyed his father and returned to school. But the boy was miserable and one morning after breakfast he left, covering the twenty-five miles to the farm on foot. Furious, Hiram threw Jim into the family's horse-drawn wagon and drove him back to school. But only minutes after his father departed, the boy defiantly struck out for home once more. This time he took an alternate route that cut about five miles from the trip and, in an amazing display of endurance, ran

almost the whole way. To Hiram's surprise, when he drove up to the house his son was waiting for him.

Discovering Football

Hiram Thorpe decided that the only way to make Jim continue his education was to enroll him in a more distant school, one he could not so easily run away from. Hiram chose Haskell Institute, an all-Indian school located in Lawrence, Kansas, hundreds of miles from the Thorpe home. Haskell had a solid reputation. It was a military-style facility that stressed manual labor and strict discipline as well as classroom instruction. Hiram felt that this would be the perfect environment for his stubborn son, and Jim Thorpe arrived at Haskell on September 17, 1898.

The boy found that his life at Haskell was busier and much more structured than it had been at the Oklahoma school. Chief Garland Nevitt of the Delaware tribe, one of Jim's friends at Haskell, later recalled:

> When Jim and I were students at Haskell, the total enrollment was more than a thousand, representing between eighty-five and ninety different tribes. It was recognized as a vocational school and was very strict because, although all the young people who wanted to attend were admitted, they were released if it was discovered that they weren't qualified. Every six months meant a change of instruction in a particular trade. This cycle was kept in effect until the individual came to the tenth grade, and then the records would show where his greatest aptitude [talent] was found, whether it was a baker, painter, blacksmith, tailor, and so forth.[10]

Although Jim Thorpe soon adjusted to the routine of school life, he did not like Haskell much better than the reservation school. However, he later fondly remembered that it was at Haskell that he was introduced to the game with which his name would be forever linked—football. According to biographer Jack Newcombe in his penetrating study of Thorpe, *The Best of the Athletic Boys:*

> Haskell acquainted him with football. The school had taken up the sport two years before he arrived and in the fall of '98 played six games, including two with Purdue and one with Denver. On the small boys' playing field Thorpe felt for the first time the sting and delight of running into a mass of tangled bodies in the crude scrimmages. Football for the small boys . . . was a matter of kicking or throwing an improvised ball around—sometimes just a stock-

ing stuffed with rags or grass and tied at the open end.[11]

Hiram Gets His Way

It was in 1900, during his second year at Haskell, that Jim Thorpe received disturbing news. His father had been wounded in a hunting accident and was said to be dying. The boy quickly jumped aboard a train that he thought was headed for Oklahoma. When he learned that the train was traveling in the wrong direction, he jumped off, sustaining a serious injury to

Thorpe on the Carlisle gridiron in 1912.

his left ankle. Yet his determination to get home and see his father before he died drove him on. In two weeks, he managed to cover more than 270 miles on foot and finally limped into the family home. Jim was surprised and delighted to see that Hiram had recovered from his illness and was his old self again.

However, only days later, the boy's delight turned to grief. His mother, who had always been in perfect health, contracted blood poisoning, or septicemia, an illness common in frontier areas with primitive sanitation, and died in the space of a week. After this tragedy, Jim was in no mood to return to school. And besides, his father now needed all the extra hands he could get to keep the farm going. So Jim Thorpe spent most of the next four years at home.

A Tradition of Good Health

Much of Jim Thorpe's excellent physical conditioning as an adult came from the lessons he learned as a child from his father and other Indian men. As Thorpe's boyhood friend Art Wakolee describes it in this excerpt from a January 1963 letter (printed in Robert W. Wheeler's Jim Thorpe: World's Greatest Athlete)*, the Indians stressed the development of both good health and sportsmanship.*

"Our people were strong and healthy in the days of our old people. The Indian system of the past was better than the one we had at school. We never received any training there. That is why Jim's father trained him when he was a young boy. His dad was known as the strongest man of his time. He taught Jim how to exercise in order to build up every part of his body. In fact, all of the young Indian men were taught the methods to keep their bodies fit and strong and clean and healthy. They were given instruction in running, jumping, wrestling, and swimming. I might add that the women also had their own health program. I know Jim's father taught him all of the clean rules for sport and life because Jim never tried to hurt anyone in football. The athletes he played with and against loved him for his good sportsmanship. Our old Chiefs gave our instructors the authority to be strict but not to use force for fear that the good competitors would be ruined. They were told not to create anger or hate in the young people they were teaching by using true kindness and love. Big Jim learned this. . . . He made our Indian people known by his good sportsmanship. I have seen Jim take a white football player's hand to show his friendship and love. . . . When he lost, he offered his hand to the victor."

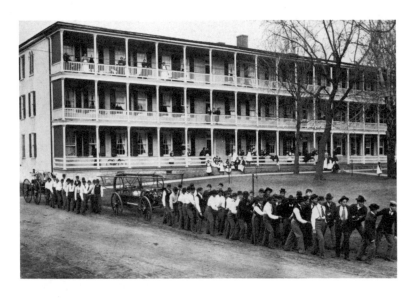

This view of the Carlisle campus shows the male students pulling fire equipment in a safety drill.

During this time, the boy and his father often did not get along. Hiram wanted Jim to continue his education, preferably at a well-known school where the boy would receive plenty of both knowledge and discipline. But Jim wanted only to stay at home. Hiram eventually got his way after hearing that a traveling superintendent from Pennsylvania's renowned Carlisle Indian School was in Oklahoma searching for recruits. In December 1903 Hiram wrote the following letter to the local Indian agent, hoping that this federal official would help get Jim enrolled. It remains unclear why Hiram claimed that fifteen-year-old Jim was only fourteen.

U.S. Indian Agent
Sac and Fox Agency OT [Oklahoma Territory]

Dear Sir—I have a boy that I wish you could Make rangements to Send of [off] to School. . . . He went to Haskill but I Think it better [for him to go to Carlisle] so he cannot run a way—he is 14 years old and I Cannot do any thing with him So plese at your Earlest Convence [convenience] atend to this for he is getting worse very [every] day—and I want him to go and make something of him Self for he cannot do it hear [here]—

Respectfully yours
Hairm Thrope
Bellmont OT

His name is James Thrope[12]

Hiram's plan succeeded. Carlisle's representative signed up his son and the boy arrived at the Pennsylvania campus in early February 1904. At the time, Jim Thorpe assumed that life at this new school would be similar to that at the others he had attended, a largely unfulfilling experience. He had no way of knowing that Carlisle would become his springboard into a fabulous sports career and into the spotlight of international fame.

2 The Rookie

Jim Thorpe's first few years at the Carlisle Indian School completely changed his life. He acquired personal discipline and a healthy respect for learning, both of which profoundly shaped his attitude. He also met many new friends. Several of the relationships he developed in these years, most especially with a remarkable coach, continued well into adulthood and helped determine the remarkable events he experienced. Most important, while at Carlisle Thorpe reached physical maturity. And he applied his unusual physical gifts to a wide range of sports activities. As a young rookie, in a relatively short time he gained mastery of football, baseball, track and field, and many other sports. He also developed a thoroughly professional attitude toward these games, which he would retain for the rest of his life.

Soaked in White Ways

When fifteen-year-old Jim Thorpe arrived at the Carlisle campus in Pennsylvania's beautiful Cumberland Valley early in 1904, he was unsure of what to expect. He knew that Carlisle was the most famous Indian school in the United States. But he did not understand how special the school was

or how lucky he was to attend it until after he had settled in and learned its history.

Carlisle, Thorpe discovered, had been established by a former Civil War officer named Richard Henry Pratt. Unlike most nineteenth-century whites, who saw Amer-

Richard Henry Pratt, Carlisle's founder, at his desk in the 1890s.

Thou Shalt Not Slug

In his book about educating the Indians, Battlefield and Classroom, *Richard Henry Pratt, Carlisle's founder, recalled a lecture he gave his Indian football players about "slugging," or intentionally hurting opponents.*

"You will never, under any circumstances, slug. . . . You will play fair straight through, and if the other fellows slug, you will in no case return it. Can't you see that if you slug, people who are looking on will say, 'There, that's the Indian of it. Just see them. They are savages and you can't get it out of them.' Our white fellows may do a lot of slugging and it causes little or no remark, but you have to make a record for your race. If the other fellows slug and you do not return it, very soon you will be the most famous football team in the country. If you can set an example of that kind for the white race, you will do a work in the highest interests of your people."

ican Indians as ignorant savages, Pratt respected and admired the Indians. While he did not consider them to be equal to whites and did little to preserve traditional Native American ways, he advocated the then-controversial idea that Indians could become contributing members of white society. The key, Pratt declared, was education. According to Jack Newcombe:

> He was certain that if he could train . . . enough Indians at enough Carlisles far removed from the influence of the reservation, the race of people might eventually be able to compete with the white man and assume an equal place in society. . . . "In Indian education I am a Baptist," Pratt said soon after coming to Carlisle, "because I believe in immersing [soaking] the Indians in our civilization, and when we get them under holding them there until they are thoroughly soaked."[13]

In 1879, after a long, uphill battle with Washington bureaucrats, Pratt succeeded in getting the government to grant him an old, run-down army barracks in the town of Carlisle, Pennsylvania. He quickly transformed the barracks into a clean, well-ordered military-style school. Pratt realized, however, that he would not continue to get public funds if he did not show some results, that is, prove that the Indians could learn white ways. So, to impress white society, he emphasized sports—an approach that would allow him to take advantage of the unusual physical conditioning and agility that so many young Indians possessed. If the Carlisle Indians could compete with and perhaps even defeat players from white schools, Pratt reasoned, people might begin to accept his theory that educating the Indians was a worthwhile endeavor. Thus, when Thorpe arrived at Carlisle, the school already had an extensive sports curriculum. And it was in the process of further expanding the size and quality of its sports programs.

Thorpe did his best to adjust to the strict regimen of school life. He found that about seven hundred Indians, ranging in age from ten to twenty-five, were enrolled; boys and girls lived in separate, two-story dormitories. The students, representing many different tribes, had to speak English at all times; they were not allowed to converse in their native tongues. Sometimes, a few students would secretly get together and speak an Indian language. If they were caught, they were punished. Verna Whistler, who taught music at Carlisle, later remembered:

The student body was self-governed. They were divided into troops and had their ranking officers just the same as the regular Army. You see the military life helped the Indians in discipline because no one was any better than the other. . . . So this system gave them a sense of order. They didn't think anything about having the same type of clothing.[14]

And Pete Calac, of Carlisle's class of 1916, recalled:

The boys wore cavalry uniforms . . . and we had the regular cavalry caps. Our shoes had to be shined at all times and especially on Saturdays when we would have inspection. . . . A bugle awakened us every morning at six o'clock and taps [bugle call signalling lights-out] were at nine in the evening. The girls had the same schedule and also had their own inspection. Breakfast was served at seven o'clock in the large dining room which accommodated the entire enrollment. It was an older building, as were most of the structures, but they were kept in good repair by students learning to be bricklayers, masons, and carpenters.[15]

At Carlisle, Indians were expected to dress, as well as speak and act, like whites, as evidenced by these photos of a young Navajo before and after enrolling at the school.

A group of Carlisle students
in their formal cavalry-style
uniforms. (Below) Thorpe
(back row, left) and his
Carlisle basketball teammates.

The Lure of Sports and Pop Warner

Thorpe was just getting used to the Carlisle regimen when he received word in April 1904 that his father had died of septicemia, the same ailment that had killed his mother. Once again, the grown-up Jim Thorpe would recall, he dealt with his grief quietly, without an outward show of emotion. He tried to forget his sorrow and loneliness by enjoying whatever sports and games he could compete in. At the time he was still too small—five feet tall and 110 pounds—to play on the varsity football and track teams. So he had to be content with the school's "shop" leagues, in which smaller, less experienced students played. Enrolled in the tailors' shop, Thorpe played football and other games in the afternoons against boys from the bakers', printers', and carpenters' shops.

Jim Thorpe also busied himself in Carlisle's "outing" program. This, like so

Coach Pop Warner (right) poses with three of his 1908 football stars: (left to right) Emil Wauseka, Jimmie Johnson, Albert Exendine.

many of the school's other programs, was designed to help young Indians learn about and fit into white society. The students were placed in temporary jobs as farmhands, laborers, and cooks in the region. Off and on during 1905 and 1906, Thorpe worked as a house cleaner and cook for five dollars a month, much less than a white youth would have received for the same job. Half these earnings went back to the school, which routinely saved them for the student worker. Young Jim Thorpe hated his outing experiences. He considered them boring and unrewarding. He wanted instead to be at school, where, he hoped, he would one day be able to work under Carlisle's renowned football and track coach, Glenn "Pop" Warner.

Pop Warner had arrived at Carlisle in 1899, after coaching for Iowa State College and the University of Georgia. In the next few years he established a reputation as one of the best coaches in the country. Later, he would be remembered as one of the greatest coaches in the history of football. According to Gregory Richards:

> Warner became famous as an innovator in football and probably did more to modernize the game than any other sportsman of his time. The double-wing formation, the spiral pass and spiral punt, and the three-point stance used by backs on the scrimmage line were all Warner innovations. He was a clever inventor as well, and during spare hours in school workshops turned out equipment such as blocking sleds, fiber padding for uniforms, and running shoes with cleats for playing on muddy fields.[16]

Warner also invented numerous plays and tactics that became standard for later college and professional players. Among

An Exceedingly Fertile Mind

Glenn "Pop" Warner, who profoundly influenced Jim Thorpe's life, was a colorful character as well as one of the greatest coaches in the history of football. In his biography of Thorpe, The Best of the Athletic Boys, *author Jack Newcombe describes Warner.*

"Warner, a 200-pounder in his late twenties with a bushy 'football' haircut, did not appear to fulfill Pratt's requisites for a teacher and molder of highly civilized men. . . . He was a hard, profane [sore] loser and drove his players without compassion. He started out by scrimmaging with them as part of their instruction but gave it up because of the injuries and wounded egos he left behind. At [the University of] Georgia [where he had coached before coming to Carlisle] he startled the candidates for the team by getting them out at six o'clock each morning for five miles of road work [running]. When he first came to Carlisle he learned to moderate his language somewhat because the Indians took his indignities [swearing at them] personally and began staying away from practice. Behind the profanity and gruffness was an exceedingly fertile mind capable of the enterprise that Pratt needed from a coach-athletic director-public relations coordinator. . . . Warner, after forty-four years as a coach . . . is remembered less for his fine teams than for his innovations. He coached from football's Stone Age into the modern era and probably had as much to do with the game's rapid evolution as anyone. The three-point sprinter's stance for backs, the blocking sled, fiber padding in uniforms, the double-wing or double-flanker formation, the cross-body block, pulling guards or tackles for interference . . . and the perfection of the spiral pass and spiral punt for accuracy and distance were some of the Warner originals or polished improvements."

Glenn "Pop" Warner.

these was a new form of blocking. Warner recalled:

> Owing to the speed and daring of the Indians, I was able to work out the "body block," a new idea. Up to that time, all blocking was done with the shoulder, a method that had a good many drawbacks. In the "Indian block," as it came to be called, a man left the ground entirely, half-turning as he leaped so as to hit an opponent just above the knees with his hip, following through with a roll, thus using his entire length. The Indians took to it like ducks to water, and when they blocked a man, he *stayed* blocked.[17]

Another Warner innovation was the infamous "hunchback play." This was a tricky, but at the time legal, move in which one of the Indian players, unbeknownst to his opponents, slipped the ball inside the back of his shirt and ran up the field, pretending only to be blocking for someone else. Pop Warner stunned the athletic world when he introduced the play against Harvard, one of the best teams in the country, in the fall of 1903. As Warner told it:

> It was up to Crimson [Harvard] to kick off. The ball sailed far and high down the center of the field, and was caught on the five-yard line by Jimmie Johnson, our little quarterback who was an All-American that year. The Indians gathered at once in what now would be called a huddle, but facing outward, and Johnson quickly slipped the ball under the back of Charlie Dillon's jersey. . . . The stands were in an uproar, for everybody had seen the big lump on Dillon's back but the Harvard players were still scurrying wildly around when Charlie crossed the goal line.[18]

Carlisle went on to defeat Penn State and other large schools with formidable reputations. This not only established Carlisle as a major force in American athletics, but also made the varsity players the heroes of the school. Jim Thorpe longed to join this select group of young Indians who were bringing credit and glory both to their school and to their race.

A Legendary Partnership Begins

Thorpe finally got his chance to meet Pop Warner in the spring of 1907. By that time the young man had filled out considerably. He was now six feet tall and weighed 185 pounds. One day he was dutifully performing one of his recently assigned daily chores—cleaning up the area of the school track near the high-jump bar. Thorpe noticed that the varsity jumpers were having trouble clearing the bar when it was set at 5 feet 9 inches. Boldly, the young man asked the jumpers if he could give it a try. Seeing that he was dressed in overalls and tennis shoes and was not even warmed up, they laughed and, convinced he would fall on his face, told him to go ahead and try. No one noticed that Pop Warner was watching curiously. To everyone's surprise and amazement, Thorpe suddenly ran full speed at the bar and sailed over it with room to spare. Warner immediately asked him to join the team for the remainder of the season. Joyfully, Thorpe accepted, marking the beginning of one of the greatest coach-player partnerships in the history of sports.

Not long afterward, Warner also recruited Thorpe for the football team. One

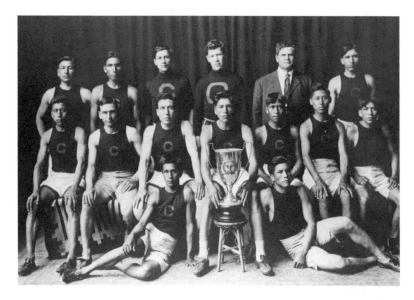

(Left) The 1909 Carlisle track team: Thorpe and Coach Warner (back row, fourth and fifth from left), Louis Tewanima (middle row, far right). (Below) Thorpe in his football outfit in 1908.

afternoon the coach noticed the young man out on the field, dressed in work clothes and plow shoes, kicking the ball around. Astounded by the great distances of the kicks, Warner asked Thorpe to play on the 1907 varsity team. On the first day of practice, the coach learned that he had acquired more than just a great kicker. During an exercise in which each player tried to run the ball past the rest of the team, Thorpe easily dodged everyone and made it to the other end of the field. To make sure it was not a fluke, Warner ordered Thorpe to try it again. Once more, in an amazing burst of speed, the young man evaded all his teammates, and Warner realized that he was watching a potentially great football player.

At the time, as talented as he was, Jim Thorpe was only one of several world-class Indian athletes at Carlisle. In the 1907 season, Warner also coached such outstanding players as Albert Exendine, Frank Mt. Pleasant, William Gardner, and Pete Hauser, one of the finest runners and kickers in the history of the game. Thorpe learned a lot from these young men as he helped them rack up an impressive string of wins.

Aiding these victories were a series of brilliant new plays by Warner. In football's early days, the game consisted mostly of running. Forward passes were not allowed. But in 1906-1907 the rules changed, allowing a certain amount of passing. Rising to the challenge, Warner invented several dazzling, never-before-seen combinations of running and passing. The resulting combination of an innovative coach and talented players proved nearly unbeatable. Carlisle defeated Villanova, Penn State, Syracuse, Bucknell, and others, and then faced their toughest challenge—the University of Pennsylvania, one of the strongest teams in the country. According to the *New York Times*:

> Playing the most remarkable football ever witnessed on Franklin Field [in Philadelphia] under the new rules, the Carlisle Indians humbled Pennsylvania this afternoon 26 to 6 in the presence of 20,000 spectators, the largest atten-

dance of the year in this city. . . . The Indians scored 16 points in the first half. . . . The entire Indian team played magnificent ball. . . . All of the Indians tackled like fiends, Penn being unable to gain through their line, around the ends or run back on punts. . . . Penn was defeated after the first five minutes of play. The Indians just swept them off their feet.[19]

Like a Genie from a Lamp

Although Thorpe had played well during the 1907 season, these games had been mainly a learning experience for him; he had not yet shown his great potential. That situation changed in the following two years. Like a mighty genie springing from a magic lamp, he unleashed his incredible athletic prowess on one unsuspecting opponent after another. First, in the 1908 track season, he electrified audiences and sportscasters by taking five first-place ribbons in each of three separate

The 1912 Carlisle football team. Thorpe is in the back row at far right.

Gentlemen All

The good sportsmanship and polite manners displayed by Carlisle's Indian athletes constantly amazed many of the whites who expected them to act like savages. In a 1931 article for Collier's *magazine entitled "Heap Big Run-Most-Fast," Pop Warner described two examples of his players' uncommonly good behavior.*

"When it comes to sportsmanship, I never want to see a finer lot of thoroughbreds than those Indians. I saw them in games against famous universities where they were slugged viciously and purposely, yet I can recall only one or two instances where an Indian repaid in kind. . . . Once Pete Hauser had to be helped off the field during a game, and when I asked him what the trouble was, he shrugged his shoulders and said, 'Same old thing. They kneed me.' 'Know who it was?' I demanded. 'Yep,' he nodded. 'Well, what did you do?' I insisted, mad all over. 'Didn't you say anything?' 'Indeed I did, Pop. Sure I said something. I said, "Who's the savage now?"'. . . In the course of my fourteen years at Carlisle, Indian football teams covered almost the whole of the United States, and I cannot recall a hotel that was not glad to have us return. Managers often remarked to me, 'They are the most gentlemanly boys we have ever had in the hotel. They are so quiet and well behaved that nobody ever knows they're around.'"

meets. One of these contests was against Syracuse, one of the strongest teams in the nation. Warner remembered:

> There seemed nothing he could not do, and whenever we needed points to win a meet, I would wait until Jim finished on the track and then throw him in the weight events [discus, shot-put, hammer throw]. The 100-yard dash, the 120- and 220-yard hurdles, the broad and high jump were his specialties, but he could also throw the hammer and put the shot with the best.[20]

Thorpe then went on to score similar triumphs in the 1908 football season. In game after game he performed spectacularly, repeatedly bringing the fans to their feet. He was so popular that during the rare times when he was on the bench, audiences loudly called for him to return. Chief Freeman Johnson, who witnessed Carlisle's game with Villanova, recalled:

> It looked as if "Pop" was never going to let Jim play. However . . . late in the second half . . . the crowd was screaming itself hoarse: "We want Jim! We want Jim!" they chanted. At long last, "Pop" tapped Jim on the shoulder and sent him in. What followed was the single most dramatic play I have ever

seen in sports. Jim took the very first hand-off and blasted into the line with the loudest crash I've ever heard. When he was able to continue into their backfield, I couldn't believe my eyes! He didn't use one block on his way to the goal line seventy yards away while all the time he kept hollering, "Out of my way! Get out of my way!"[21]

Pop Warner best summed up Thorpe's tremendous abilities during these years, saying:

No college player I ever saw had the natural aptitude for football possessed by Jim Thorpe. I never knew a football player who could penetrate a line as Thorpe could, nor did I ever know of a player who could see holes through which to break as could the big Indian. As for speed, none ever carried a pigskin down the field with the dazzling speed of Thorpe. He could go skidding through first and second defense, knock off a tackler, stop short and turn past another, ward off still another, and escape the entire pack; or, finally cornered, could go farther with a tackler [hanging on] than any man I ever knew. He knew everything a football player could be taught and then he could execute the play better than the coach ever dreamed of.[22]

A Fateful Summer

In the spring of 1909, Thorpe continued his successes in track and field. He had become so proficient at so many events that Warner felt it unnecessary to field a large team. For example, against neighboring Lafayette College, Thorpe and six teammates defeated a squad of more than forty athletes by a score of 71 to 41. This was a formidable accomplishment. The sides scored a certain number of team points for each first-, second-, or third-place win. To ensure as many of these wins as possible, most teams fielded a specialist for each event, an athlete who had the advantage of spending all his time training for a single event. Thorpe delivered a spectacular performance, competing in an unprecedented seven events and winning six first places and a third place.

After the track season ended, Thorpe decided to accept an offer by some friends to join them in playing minor-league baseball during the summer. This certainly appealed to him much more than taking another boring outing job. Although he had only minimal experience in baseball, he was an excellent player and enjoyed the game. He soon found a team in Rocky Mount, North Carolina, that offered him fifteen dollars a week. This was just enough to cover his living expenses while away from Carlisle. That summer, he played in towns up and down the East Coast, acting as a pitcher in several games, and batted a respectable average of .253. Thorpe enjoyed himself thoroughly. But as it turned out, his decision to play summer baseball was a fateful one. Little did he realize that this seemingly innocent diversion would one day become a controversial scandal that would cause him tremendous grief and embarrassment.

3 The Olympian

After his summer of minor-league baseball, Jim Thorpe decided not to return to Carlisle in the fall of 1909. He missed seeing his home and his brothers and sisters and spent much of the following two years on the family farm in Oklahoma. But the time away from school was far less satisfying than he had imagined it would be. He had grown accustomed to the busy routine of school life and the thrill of competing in track and football. Eventually, some of his former teammates convinced him to return to Carlisle. Thorpe's return to the school in the fall of 1911 turned out be a strategic one, not only for himself, but also for Carlisle. He proceeded to lead his teammates to a string of impressive victories on the playing fields, once more establishing the Indian school as one of the dominant forces in American sports. And he also carved for himself a slice of immortality. With Pop Warner's help, Thorpe trained for and competed in the 1912 Olympics, gaining international recognition as the greatest all-around athlete in the world.

The Legend Begins to Grow

Thrilled to have Thorpe back on his football team, Pop Warner built much of his

Thorpe (far right) poses with some of his Carlisle football teammates.

No Foundation in Fact

Carlisle's monthly student publication, The Red Man by Red Men, *tried to promote a better image for Native Americans. This excerpt from a 1911 issue criticizes the way early motion pictures were misrepresenting Indians, especially by having people of other races play Indian roles.*

"[We take issue with the] untrue and libelous brand of moving pictures of Indian life and romance which are shown throughout the country, and are supposed by the uninitiated public to be true to life. . . . The majority of these pictures are not only without foundation in fact, but do not even have Indians to pose for them. . . . White men or Mexicans usually pose as Indians, with blackened faces, wigs, and Indian costume; their actions and gestures are absurdly grotesque, and exaggerated. These make-believes do not run, talk, or walk like Indians, and their whole make-up brands them as 'fakers.'. . . [Such presentations] tend to create hostility against the Indian among many of his friends, and to alienate many white people."

1911 offensive strategy around him. In game after game that season, Thorpe ran, kicked, and blocked better than he ever had, and his legend continued to grow around the country. After Carlisle's crushing 17-0 victory over the University of Pittsburgh, the *Pittsburgh Leader* commented:

> To say Thorpe is the whole team would be fifty percent wrong, but he certainly is the most consistent performer. . . . His returning of punts, line-bucking, fake plays, and other maneuvers getting him great applause.[23]

The *Pittsburgh Dispatch* also lauded Thorpe:

> This person Thorpe is a host in himself. Tall and sinewy, as quick as a flash and as powerful as a turbine engine, he appeared to be impervious [immune] to injury. Kicking from 50 to 70

yards every time his shoe crashed against the ball, he seemed possessed of superhuman speed, for whenever the pigskin alighted, there he was, ready either to grab it or to down the Pitt player who secured it. At line-bucking and general all-around work, this Sac and Fox shone resplendent [magnificent] and then some.[24]

The Carlisle team went on to defeat many other teams, including Harvard, then the game's defending national champion, and Brown University in Rhode Island. In the Brown game, during which his friend Gus Welch made a stunning sixty-two-yard touchdown run, Thorpe kicked two big field goals. One was twenty-seven yards and the other thirty-three, distances at which kicking accurately was difficult. Thorpe also booted an incredible eighty-three-yard punt, setting a new collegiate record. At the time, punts of sixty to seventy yards were considered first rate. So impressive was his overall performance that season that sports writers all over the country sang his praises, making him a household name. One writer recognized that Thorpe was more than just a fine football player, saying:

> The 1911 football season has brought into the public eye a young Indian student at the Carlisle School who is the most versatile athlete ever known. Thorpe is at present playing on the Indian football team and is considered one of the best halfbacks in the history of the game.[25]

Training for the Olympics

Thorpe's fellow students also held him in high esteem. At the end of the 1911 season his football teammates elected him team captain. And, as the undisputed hero of the school, he began receiving a great deal of attention from female students. That fall he met eighteen-year-old Iva Miller, a Scotch-Irish Cherokee from Oklahoma, who was about to graduate with honors. For Iva, their first date proved a bit disconcerting. The twenty-three-year-old Thorpe started the evening off by innocently but rather awkwardly exclaiming, "You're a cute little thing." Nevertheless, they hit it off, continued to date, and grew ever closer over the following winter and spring.

In addition to Iva, Thorpe had much to occupy his time during these months. Pop Warner was confident that Thorpe

and Hopi Louis Tewanima, a gifted long-distance runner, were talented enough to try out for the U.S. Olympic team. The 1912 games, the fifth cycle of the modern era, were scheduled to begin in the summer in Stockholm, Sweden. That meant there was no time to lose in preparing the two athletes. Warner knew that the best possible training was actual competition, so he used Thorpe and Tewanima to spearhead his 1912 track team. That season Thorpe won numerous first-place medals. Some of his best events were the 100-yard dash, the 45-, 120-, and 220-yard hurdles, the standing broad jump, the high jump, and the shot put. In a single three-way meet involving Carlisle, the University of Pennsylvania, and Carnegie

Iva Miller, whom Thorpe met and dated at Carlisle.

Technical School, Thorpe won three first places, two second, and a third. Thanks to spectacular performances by himself and Tewanima, Carlisle scored 82 points, while the other two teams racked up only 32 points each.

Both Thorpe and Tewanima easily qualified for the Olympics at the tryouts in late spring. Their excitement mounted as they counted down the days to their de-

Thorpe trains aboard the S.S. Finland *on the way to the Stockholm Olympics.*

parture on the S.S. *Finland* with the other 162 members of the U.S. Olympic team. On June 14, 1912, the two nervous athletes, accompanied by Pop Warner, boarded the huge luxury liner in New York City. Thorpe was immediately surprised and impressed by the sheer size of the vessel. As Jack Newcombe tells it:

> Nothing that Thorpe was to experience at the Games in Stockholm was to prove more awesome than his discovery of the size and accommodations of the *Finland*. His traveling companions, Louis Tewanima and Pop Warner, acting as trainer and appointed chaperone for the two Indian wards, had encountered the wonders of ocean voyaging before. Thorpe was overwhelmed. Years later he said that boarding and touring the boat remained with him as the largest thrill of the Olympic trip. "I'd never seen a boat as big as that before. I've seen a lot since. But nothing was like that—walking on the boat, and all those cabins and the decks and eating and sleeping on it."[26]

In the years that followed Thorpe's participation in the Olympics, a number of popular stories circulated about how he had refused to train either on the ship or in Stockholm before the games opened. Most of these stories were based on an anecdote related by U.S. marathoner Johnny Hayes, who later claimed:

> One day I looked out from our quarters in Stockholm and saw Jim get out of a hammock and walk to the sidewalk. I saw him mark off about 23 feet. I thought he was going to do some jumping and was shocked at the idea he would try it on the pavement. He

walked back to the hammock and climbed in, eyeing the two marks. For all I could see, that was the training he did for the broad jump.[27]

Assuming this story is factual, Hayes had to have misinterpreted the situation. In fact, Thorpe had always trained hard for upcoming contests, and the Olympics, the most prestigious of all, would hardly have been an exception. This view is amply supported by the testimony of many eyewitnesses. According to Avery Brundage, former president of the International Olympic Committee and Thorpe's teammate at the time:

> Certainly Thorpe trained and never missed a session! Even if he, or anyone else for that matter had wanted to loaf, our trainer, Mike Murphy, would not have permitted it. Jim's own coach, "Pop" Warner, was hand-picked by Murphy to take great pains to ensure that Thorpe and Tewanima . . . would be in perfect condition.[28]

A Display of Versatility

And indeed, that summer Thorpe was at the peak of his physical conditioning. He weighed 181 pounds, had a 40-inch chest, a 32-inch waist, a 16-inch neck, a 73-inch reach, and not a single ounce of excess body fat. He had to be in the best shape possible because he was to compete in the two most comprehensive and grueling contests of the games. The first was the Pentathlon, a series of five events: 200-meter run, 1500-meter run, broad jump, discus throw, and javelin throw. Whereas most competitors have to be proficient in only one kind of activity, a pentathlete

Gifted distance runner Louis Tewanima in his Carlisle track uniform.

must be physically versatile. And versatility was Thorpe's strongest attribute.

The Pentathlon was held in Stockholm's crowded Olympic stadium on July 7. Thorpe's magnificent performance surprised and amazed most of the European spectators, who fully expected a Swede or other European to capture the Pentathlon gold. At the time, Europeans were considered to be the best all-around athletes, while Americans had a reputation for specializing in single events. The stadium audience watched with growing awe and

Thorpe in one of his Olympic uniforms (left), and throwing the javelin in the Pentathlon.

respect as the muscular American Indian handily won four out of the five events. As Gregory Richards describes it:

> Competition in the Pentathlon began with the broad jump. In the photographs, one can see the perfect form Thorpe showed in his jump. His arms were high in the air and his legs curled beneath him at a right angle to his body. He sailed 23 feet 2.7 inches, which beat the rest of the contenders. He didn't throw the javelin quite as successfully, placing third with a throw of just under 153 feet 3 inches, as compared with the winner's mark of 162 feet 7 inches. Failing to take first place in that event may have been what compelled Jim to outperform his competitors in the remaining three events. He hurled the discus 116 feet 8.4 inches, three feet farther than his United States teammate, Avery Brundage. He

edged out two other Americans in the 200-meter dash . . . and he stunned spectators with a wide-lead finish in the 1500-meter race, clocking a time of 4 minutes 44.8 seconds and leaving the others many feet behind.[29]

Even the U.S. officials were pleasantly surprised at Thorpe's performance. They had felt that he had a good chance at winning a medal in the Pentathlon, but had not dreamed he would take four of the five events. James Sullivan, head of the Amateur Athletic Union, or AAU, the group that sponsored the United States at the Olympics and other international competitions, remarked that Thorpe's all-around work "was certainly sensational. It answers the charge that Americans specialize in athletics. It also answers the allegation that most of our runners are of foreign parentage for Thorpe [being an Indian] is a real American if there ever was one."[30]

But Thorpe had just begun to show what he could do. As difficult and demanding as the Pentathlon had been, it constituted only a foretaste of his next challenge, the physically grueling Decathlon. The ultimate test of all-around athletic prowess, the Decathlon is composed of ten events: 100-meter run, broad jump, shot put, high jump, 400-meter run, 110-meter high hurdles, discus throw, pole vault, javelin throw, and 1500-meter run. In each event, each competitor receives points, the amounts based on the quality of his performance in comparison to his opponents'. The competitor with the highest number of points at the end of the contest wins. At the time, the ten events were staged over a three-day period.

In the Stockholm games, six days separated the Pentathlon and Decathlon contests. During the interval, Thorpe did his best to prepare himself physically and mentally for the challenge that lay ahead. He also happily watched his teammate and friend Louis Tewanima capture second place and a silver medal in the 10,000-meter race.

The Decathlon began on July 13 with the 100-meter dash. Both Thorpe and Pop Warner were disappointed with Thorpe's performance. He had run the distance in an impressive 9.8 seconds in a practice sprint. But in the actual competition, he ran it in 11.2 seconds, placing only third. Next came the running broad jump, in which Thorpe did better, placing second with a jump of 22 feet 2.3 inches. Both Thorpe and Warner knew that the next event, the shot put, was one of the Indian's strongest. Sure enough, Thorpe brought the people in the stands to their feet, mightily heaving the heavy iron ball 42 feet 5.5 inches. This easily gave him first place in the event and at the end of

Thorpe puts the shot, taking first place in the event, on the first day of the Decathlon.

The runners, including Thorpe (second from left), leave their marks at the start of the 1500-meter run, final event of the grueling Decathlon.

the first day he led his opponents with an overall total of 2,544.75 points.

The next day, Thorpe continued his lead. In the opening event, the high jump, he thrilled spectators and opponents alike with an incredible first-place leap of 6 feet 1.6 inches. Although his performance in the 400-meter run was less impressive, he managed to run the distance in 47.6 seconds for fourth place. Then came the 110-meter hurdles, one of Thorpe's strongest events. In a stunning combination of speed, strength, and agility, he delivered a performance that would live long both in onlookers' memories and in the record books. As Robert Wheeler put it:

The best way to describe Jim's time of 15.6 seconds is to compare it with [U.S. decathlete] Bob Mathias's mark of

15.7 seconds in the 1948 Olympics in London. Thirty-six years of onslaught, involving improved diets, training procedures, hurdling techniques, and equipment had not been able to break track's longest-standing record.[31]

Thorpe entered the final day of Decathlon competition with a commanding lead of 5,302.87 points. He managed to keep this lead by continuing to rack up first-, second-, and third-place scores. He took second place in the discus with a heave of 121 feet 4 inches, third in the javelin with a throw of 149 feet 11 inches, and third in the pole vault with a jump of 10 feet 8 inches. After his tremendous output of physical exertion in nine events over three days, most people expected Thorpe to be too exhausted to do well in the final 1500-meter run. Yet he surprised everyone again by besting the time of his 1500-meter Pentathlon run by more than 4 seconds. His completion of the distance in 4 minutes 40.1 seconds climaxed his bravura three-day display of athletic greatness with another first-place win. And he emerged as the winner of the Decathlon, with an overall point total of 8,412.96, a record that would stand for twenty years.

That same afternoon, the medals and honors for the Pentathlon, Decathlon, and other events were presented. Sweden's King Gustav handed out the awards for the first-place winners. When it was his turn, Thorpe, now dressed in a tie and

Debunking the Myth of Specialization

Until Thorpe's great performance at the 1912 Olympics, most sports authorities held that U.S. athletes were good at individual events but less capable than Europeans as all-around athletes. After the Stockholm games, AAU official James Sullivan made this statement, which was recorded by Thorpe in his personal scrapbook (here quoted in Robert W. Wheeler's Jim Thorpe: World's Greatest Athlete*).*

"The field events at the Olympic Games comprised the usual standard events: hammer, shot, discus, pole vault, javelin, high and broad jumps, in which events the American athletes again demonstrated their superiority, but the Swedes had two events on the programme never held heretofore [before], the Pentathlon and Decathlon. These two events were added to the Olympic Games in Sweden to give the world a chance to see the type of athlete that comes from countries that believe in all-around excellence, the claim having been made that certain nations—especially America—specialized, some in sprinting, some in jumping, throwing the weights, etc. The work of our men in the two all-around competitions, the Decathlon and Pentathlon, and the showing of James Thorpe, the winner of them, should forever remove from any doubting minds the impression that Americans specialized for one event. Thorpe's record has not been equaled and will not be equaled for many years [a prediction that proved accurate]. And Thorpe had a reputation in other lines of sport long before he began to attract attention in track and field athletics, for besides being a splendid baseball player, he is a star lacrosse player and has the honor of being selected by the leading authority on football in America, Mr. Walter Camp, as a member of the blue ribbon-though-mythical team, the 'All-American Football Team.'"

Thorpe (left), wearing the victor's laurel wreath, stands before Sweden's King Gustav (on podium).

jacket, proudly stood triumphant before the king, and, in a sense, before the world. The *New York Times* reported:

> When James Thorpe, the Carlisle Indian and finest all-around athlete in the world, appeared to claim the prizes for winning the Pentathlon, there was a great burst of cheers, led by the king. The immense crowd cheered itself hoarse.[32]

For his Pentathlon win, Thorpe received the Olympic gold medal, a victor's laurel wreath, and a four-foot-high bronze bust of King Gustav. The awards for the Decathlon included another gold medal and wreath, and also a silver cup lined with gold and precious jewels and shaped like a Viking ship. Taking Thorpe's hand, the king, his voice quavering with emotion, declared, "Sir, you are the greatest athlete in the world!" Thorpe's quiet, simple, and modest reply was, "Thanks, King."[33]

In addition to his medals and trophies, Thorpe received many words of praise from people around the world. But per-haps the honor he was most proud of was a letter from William H. Taft, the president of the United States, who wrote:

> I have much pleasure in congratulating you on account of your noteworthy victory at the Olympic Games in Stockholm. Your performance is one of which you may well be proud. You have set a high standard of physical development which is only attained by right living and right thinking, and your victory will serve as an incentive to all to improve these qualities which characterize the best type of American citizen.[34]

Only a few decades before, the U.S. government had been engaged in the systematic destruction of the "inferior" Native American race. Now, that government's highest official was thanking a member of that race for being a superior physical specimen and a model citizen. It was an ironic turn of events, one which brought tears of pride to the eyes of many Indians across the United States that summer.

4 The Example

In August 1912 shortly following their participation in the Stockholm Olympics, Thorpe, Tewanima, and Pop Warner returned to Carlisle in a blaze of glory. Arthur Martin, the secretary of the school's athletic department, later recalled the huge, happy celebration:

> They had bands and different games, and more than 15,000 people turned out to welcome him [Thorpe]. They had a speaking stand, upon which several people got up and made various speeches about all that Thorpe, Warner, and Tewanima had accomplished.

Jim was asked to make a speech and so he went up and acknowledged the affair and made a very nice speech. The people really enjoyed seeing and hearing him.[35]

The Carlisle tribute was only the first of many. The following week in New York City, he, along with other fellow Olympians, rode for hours down Fifth Avenue as more than a million people cheered. And similar celebrations followed in Boston and Philadelphia. On these occasions, hundreds of people lined up to shake Thorpe's hand or get his autograph.

Thorpe and Tewanima ride in triumph in Carlisle, Pennsylvania's post-Olympic homecoming victory parade.

(Above) Thorpe's and Tewanima's victory carriage enters the Carlisle town square. (Below) Carlisle's Mayor William J. Gaynor congratulates Thorpe at the climax of the victory parade.

And dozens of promoters approached him, offering him jobs in traveling side shows and on well-known baseball teams.

Overwhelmed by all this attention, Thorpe was happy to get back to the familiar surroundings of Carlisle. Pop Warner had convinced him to stay long enough to complete his studies and graduate before going on to bigger and better things. In the meantime, the school would benefit by having the Olympic champion on the football team for one more season.

Perhaps Warner cannot be blamed for wanting to hang onto his famous protégé for as long as possible. Warner was well aware that with Thorpe leading the team, the school would once more be one of the strongest football threats in the nation. Thorpe was then in the peak condition of his life and, from a physical and emotional standpoint, almost a perfect football player. Syracuse player Joseph Alexander, a frequent Carlisle opponent, described Thorpe at the time:

He had terrific flexibility and his coordination was absolutely beautiful. He was not powerful in the sense that he had so much strength, it was his coordination that made him strong. His movements were all easy, simple, and flexible, and most important of all, he never played football with any anxiety or fear or anything to hinder his mind from acting on a split second's notice.[36]

And to the continued amazement of teammates and opponents alike, Thorpe excelled at practically any sport he tried. Despite rarely having the time to play either game, he could consistently bowl in the 200s and shoot golf in the 70s. He also showed remarkable talent and skill in lacrosse, tennis, handball, rowing, hockey, billiards, and figure skating. The title of "world's best all-around athlete" fit Jim Thorpe perhaps better than any other sports figure in history.

Like Clutching a Shadow

Thorpe's great athletic abilities were tested anew in the 1912 football season. As crowds showered him with ovations, he led the Indian team to victory after victory. Carlisle crushed Syracuse 33–0, then went on to defeat Pittsburgh 45–8, Georgetown

Carlisle's legendary 1912 football team, with Captain Thorpe and Coach Warner (back row, third and fourth from left).

A Superhuman Player

Jim Thorpe inspired praise, not only from his friends, but also from his opponents. This statement printed in Jim Thorpe: World's Greatest Athlete *by Robert W. Wheeler, is from Leland Devore, West Point's great football lineman who played against Thorpe.*

"That Indian is the greatest player I have ever stacked up against in my five years experience. He is superhuman, that is all. There is no stopping him. Talk about your Ted Coys! Why this Indian is as far ahead of the great Yale back as Coy is ahead of a prep-school player. Thorpe smashes into the line like a pair of Coys. There is nothing he can't do. He kicks superbly, worms his way through a field like a combination of grey-hound, jackrabbit, and eel. He is as cunning and strategic as a fox. He follows interference like the hangers-on follow an army. You may have your Lefty Flynns, Brickleys, Bakers, and Coys [for lists of the greatest players], but Thorpe for mine every time."

34–20, and Lehigh 34–14. In the Lehigh game, Thorpe thrilled spectators by single-handedly scoring 28 of his team's 34 points.

All the while, the Carlisle players mentally prepared themselves for their upcoming November 9 game against the Army players of West Point. For the Indians, this was to be more than just a physical contest. Pop Warner regularly reminded them that their fathers and grandfathers had once faced off against the forebears of the Army players in a real and bloody conflict. Now, that past rivalry would be revived on the playing field. Here, said Warner, was the chance for the Indians to prove that in a fair fight they could beat the best the U.S. government could throw at them.

Rising to this challenge, Thorpe and his teammates ran onto the West Point field and played their hearts out. The Army cadets were equally eager to prove themselves superior, and the result was one of the hardest-played, most exciting football games in history. Reported the *New York Times*:

Standing out resplendent in a galaxy of Indian stars was Jim Thorpe, recently crowned the athletic marvel of the age. The big Indian Captain added more luster [shine] to his already brilliant record, and at times the game itself was almost forgotten while the spectators gazed on Thorpe, the individual, to wonder at his prowess. To recount his notable performances in the complete overthrow of the Cadets would leave little space for other notable points of the conflict. He simply ran wild, while the Cadets tried in vain to stop his progress. It was like trying to clutch a shadow. Thorpe went through the West Point line as if it was an open door; his defensive play was on a par with his attack and his every move was that of a past master. . . . West Point's much-talked-of defense . . . was like tissue paper before the Indians. To a corresponding degree the Indian defense, which had been considered so much inferior to their attack, was a wonder.[37]

To Pop Warner's delight, his players completely outplayed the Army cadets and decisively beat West Point by a score of 27–6. But though all the Indian players

Future president Dwight Eisenhower as a West Point football star in 1912.

had performed well, everyone knew that the victory had been spearheaded by Jim Thorpe. On that day he earned the respect of some of his greatest adversaries. After the game, West Point's 6-foot 3-inch, 200-pound Leland Devore, one of the best collegiate linemen in football history, said of Thorpe, "That Indian is the greatest player I have ever stacked up against in my five years experience. He is superhuman, that is all."[38] Another cadet who played that day was Dwight Eisenhower, who would become the thirty-fourth president of the United States. Remembering Thorpe, Eisenhower later said, "On the football field, there was no one like him in the world. Against us, he dominated all of the action."[39] Indeed, Thorpe dominated nearly every game he played that season. In all, he scored an impressive 198 points, a new collegiate season point total.

Unwise in the Ways of the World

It was at the season's conclusion, just as he had reached his height of achievement and popularity, that a controversial story about Thorpe broke in the newspapers. The events leading up to the scandal had begun late in 1912. While Thorpe and his teammates were playing some practice scrimmages in Worcester, Massachusetts, some local sports officials and reporters dropped by to watch. Among them was Roy Johnson, a reporter for the *Worcester Telegram*. When he began conversing with a baseball manager from a neighboring town, the manager suddenly exclaimed that he recognized Thorpe. As it happened, the man had formerly managed one of the North Carolina minor-league baseball teams that Thorpe had played for a few years before.

Johnson realized that he had a potentially big story on his hands. At the time, the International Olympic Committee, or IOC, the U.S. AAU, and other leading sports organizations insisted that all Olympic athletes be amateurs. This meant that they could not accept money for competing. The rule was partly designed to make it fairer for inexperienced athletes by keeping more seasoned professionals out of the games. But at the time the main reason for the rule was a belief by most athletic officials and leaders that taking money somehow corrupted athletes. According to this view, amateurs were "purer" athletes than professionals. Since Thorpe had played baseball for money, he had not been an amateur when he competed in the Olympics. The IOC and AAU, Johnson reasoned, would hold that Thorpe had won his medals under false pretenses.

Johnson broke his story in the *Worcester Telegram* on January 23, 1913, and within two days nearly every major newspaper in the world carried headlines about Thorpe taking money. Thorpe felt both confused and humiliated. He maintained that when he had accepted the expense money he had been completely unaware that it was wrong. Official reaction was unsympathetic, however. The AAU's James Sullivan called for a hearing to discuss bringing charges of professionalism against Thorpe. Warned Sullivan:

If he is found to have broken the rules as stated, he will be stripped of all his records, his name taken from the athletic annuals, and he will be compelled to return all the prizes he has won since his infraction of the rules.[40]

Pop Warner and other friends advised Thorpe to write a letter to the AAU admitting what he had done, explaining his ignorance of any wrongdoing, and asking for forgiveness. Thorpe agreed and wrote to Sullivan on January 27. The letter said in part:

I played baseball at Rocky Mount and at Fayetteville, N.C., in the summer of 1909 and 1910 under my own name. On the same teams I played with were several college men from the north who were earning money by ball playing during vacations and who were regarded as amateurs at home. I did not play for the money there was in it . . . but because I liked to play ball. I was not wise in the ways of the world and did not realize this was wrong, and that it would make me a professional in track sports, although I learned from the other players that it would be better for me not to let anyone know that I was playing and for that reason I never told anyone at the school about it until today. . . . I have always liked sports and only played or run races for the fun of the things and never to earn money. . . . I am very sorry, Mr. Sullivan, to have it all spoiled in this way and I hope the Amateur Athletic Union and the people will not be too hard in judging me.[41]

The AAU Blasted

But the AAU did indeed judge Jim Thorpe harshly. The organization was embar-

The AAU's Stern Action

In rejecting Jim Thorpe's apology for playing baseball for money, the AAU made a public statement (quoted partially here from Robert W. Wheeler's Jim Thorpe: World's Greatest Athlete).

"The Team Selection Committee of the American Olympic Committee selected James Thorpe as one of the members of the American Olympic team, and did so without the least suspicion as to there having been any act of professionalism on Thorpe's part. . . . The widest possible publicity was given of the team selected . . . and it seems strange that men having knowledge of Thorpe's professional conduct did not at such time, for the honor of their country, come forward and place in the hands of the American Committee such information as they had. No such information was given as to Thorpe being other than the amateur which he was supposed to be. Thorpe's act of professionalism was in a sport over which the Amateur Athletic Union has no direct control. . . . The reason why he himself did not give notice of his acts is explained by him on the ground of ignorance. . . . The American Olympic Committee and the Amateur Athletic Union tender to the Swedish Olympic Committee, and through the International Olympic Committee, to the nations of the world, their apology for having entered Thorpe and having permitted him to compete at the Olympic Games of 1912. The Amateur Athletic Union regrets that it permitted Thorpe to compete in amateur contests during the past several years, and will do everything in its power to secure the return of prizes and readjustment of points won by him, and will immediately eliminate his records from the books."

rassed over the scandal and, despite the Indian's honesty and sincerity, it decided to make an example of him. In a public statement, the AAU claimed that it had no knowledge of Thorpe's having played professional baseball at the time it sponsored him for the Olympics. The AAU condemned Thorpe's action and apologized to the IOC and to the world community for allowing him to compete. In addition, the organization echoed Sullivan's earlier call for Thorpe to return his awards and again promised to eliminate his records from the Olympic books.

Public reaction was swift, and, almost unanimously, against the AAU's action.

Across the country and around the world, sports and editorial writers, and many fans as well, angrily asked why the AAU had singled out Thorpe. It was well known, they pointed out, that many young college athletes regularly played summer sports for expense money. The popular sentiment seemed to be that this hardly constituted professionalism. And what about the many college officials who paid young athletes' expenses to get them to attend their schools? Was that not the same sort of thing and, therefore, a practice the AAU should also be denouncing? An editorial in the *Philadelphia Times* blasted the AAU, saying that it

> should feel proud over its accomplishment in "purifying" athletics by disgracing Thorpe and kicking up a

muss that will be heralded the world over as a disgrace to this country. All aspiring athletes will do well to ponder this action of the [AAU] and not play croquet, ping-pong, tiddly winks, or button-button-who's-got-the-button for compensation. It puts them in the ranks of professionals and absolutely disqualifies them from being able to run, jump, hurdle, throw the discus, pole vault, or wrestle. What will it [the AAU] do with the college athletes that are given their tuition free, and made the recipient of special favors "on the side," in order that their services on the football field and in track events may be utilized? . . . There is every reason to believe that the Amateur Athletic Union knew of many such instances, but winked at them.[42]

Jim Thorpe's 1912 Olympic medals.

As Fair as Digging Ditches

Many newspapers around the world disagreed with or denounced the AAU for its severe punishment of Jim Thorpe. This particularly critical statement (from Thorpe's personal scrapbook and quoted by Robert W. Wheeler in Jim Thorpe: World's Greatest Athlete*) was made by the* Buffalo Enquirer.

"Jim Thorpe, amateur or no amateur, is the greatest athlete today in the world. They can take away his tin medals and his pieces of pottery and they can hold him up to the scorn of a few 'pure athletes,' but the honest world, the thinking world, the great majority of men and women will always consider him the athlete par excellence of the past fifty years in this country. AAU officials think nothing of taking money for their services as managers of athletic meets at the various world's expositions; still the men at the head of this AAU, who accept thousands of dollars, are so 'pure' that they cannot be approached. To talk of that bunch as 'money getters' would be lèse majesté [high treason], but the fact is becoming more evident every day that the people of this country refuse to accept the judgment of this clique as to the athletic standing of a man. In Thorpe's case he played ball one summer for a few months. It was three years ago when he was attending a preparatory school. Other college men did the same thing. Instead of hanging around all summer grafting pin money [bumming spending money] from their hard working parents they went out and worked for their living playing baseball, earning a living that way, which is as fair a way as if they had been digging ditches or working on a farm pitching hay."

The *Toronto Mail and Empire* also came out in support of Thorpe:

> The rest of the world . . . will decline to see any great difference between a man running a race and receiving twenty or fifty dollars for his efforts, and a man running a race and receiving a gold watch [or medal] worth twenty or fifty dollars. . . . In fact, the rest of the world . . . is inclined to regard the distinction between amateurism and professionalism as the modern counterpart of the distinction between Tweedledum and Tweedledee [twin characters from Lewis Carroll's *Through the Looking Glass*].[43]

And the *Buffalo Enquirer* declared emphatically, "Jim Thorpe, amateur or no amateur, is the greatest athlete today in the world."[44]

A Wound That Never Healed

But despite almost universal condemnation, the AAU refused to change its ruling. Thorpe would be required to return his medals and trophies. He said later that when he and Warner packed up and mailed the gold medals and trophies to the Olympic Committee in February 1913 it was one of his most difficult duties. The awards were to be given to Norway's F.R. Bie and Sweden's Hugo Wieslander, the men who had placed second to him in the Pentathlon and Decathlon, respectively. It was one of the low points of Thorpe's life. His spirits brightened slightly, however, when he heard that Bie and Wieslander had refused to accept the prizes. In a gallant gesture, Wieslander sent the package back to the Olympic Committee unopened, along with a note saying, "I didn't win the Olympic Decathlon. James Thorpe did. I don't know what your rules are in regard to amateurism, but I do know, having competed against him, that Thorpe is the greatest athlete in the world."[45]

Thorpe now tried as best he could to put the affair behind him. The scandal had embarrassed and saddened him but it differed from prior tragedies in his life because he had not had to bear the hurt in anguished silence. This time he had received much sympathy and support from his siblings, teammates, Pop Warner, and Iva, whom he was still dating. Their support enabled him to keep his dignity and sense of humor. Yet for the rest of his life being made an example by the AAU remained a wound that never quite healed. Years later, Chief Meyers, a baseball player and Thorpe's friend, recalled:

I remember, very late one night, Jim came in and woke me up. I remember it like it was only last night. He was crying, and tears were rolling down his cheeks. "You know, Chief," he said, "the King of Sweden gave me those trophies, he gave them to me. But they took them away from me. They're mine, Chief, I won them fair and square." It broke his heart, and he never fully recovered.[46]

5 The Professional

After the trauma of losing his Olympic prizes, Jim Thorpe's life went in a completely new direction. This was partly because he realized that he needed to do something different, something that would help him put the unhappy affair behind him. But even without the scandal, his life would have changed soon anyway. He was in his last few months at Carlisle. He had spent more than seven of the preceding nine years of his life at the school, which had become like a home to him. Yet he knew that the time had finally come to leave school's sheltered life and earn a living in the "real" world.

For years there had been little doubt in Thorpe's mind as to the type of career he would pursue. He was already the most famous athlete in the world; the only logical choice was professional sports. But what sport should he choose? Thorpe preferred football, but at the time professional football was in its infancy and had not become the well-organized, well-paying sport it is today. So at first he chose baseball, ironically the very sport that had gotten him into so much trouble. Yet, despite honest effort and hard work, great success in baseball seemed to elude him. And all the while the dream of playing football remained strong. Eventually, Thorpe would turn his dream of professional football

into reality, not only for himself, but for generations of players to come. And in doing so, he would add a new dimension to his own growing legend.

A Name That Sold Tickets

Once Thorpe had decided to go into professional baseball, the next order of business was to choose a team. And with his reputation, he had plenty to choose from. In the spring of 1913 at least half a dozen major-league teams offered him contracts. What appeared to be the best offer came from the world champion New York Giants. Its manager, John J. McGraw, offered Thorpe $5,000 for a one-year contract, at the time a huge sum of money even for a seasoned veteran, let alone a new player. The twenty-five-year-old American Indian felt it would be foolish to turn down so much money and a chance to play with the best ball club in the world. So he accepted McGraw's offer.

However, this, the first of Thorpe's professional job choices, turned out to be a mistake. He had assumed that being an athletic celebrity, he would get to play a lot of baseball. In reality, McGraw had indeed hired him because of his fame, but

Not a Thorpe in the Lot

One professional sport that Thorpe did not try was boxing. But many sportswriters and promoters felt that he had the makings of a champion prizefighter. This New York World *editorial, quoted in Robert W. Wheeler's* Jim Thorpe: World's Greatest Athlete, *was typical of many pieces that recognized his potential as a boxer.*

"Imagine what Jim would do if he were turned loose among the heavyweights! Six feet tall and heavy in proportion, Thorpe has the height and reach of a champion. He is amazingly strong. He could fight a hundred rounds without breaking down, if necessary. This is shown by his phenomenal endurance in athletics, which enabled him to win both the Pentathlon and Decathlon in Stockholm. Moreover Thorpe can take any amount of battering. And here we have the most important fighting characteristic he possesses. Everyone knows that there's no sport in the world better than boxing for developing self-control. That's because self-control is absolutely necessary to the boxer. Without it he has no more chance to win than a nerve-shaken sharpshooter has to hit the bull's-eye. Look at the photograph of Thorpe's face. You can see, unhidden by the massive chin and neck and the high cheek bones and keen eyes, unbounded good nature combined with unlimited courage and determination and aggressiveness. . . . I've seen many a good man go out for the heavyweight title and a few good men land it. But there wasn't a Thorpe in the lot."

not necessarily to play the game. The manager was much more interested in the power of Thorpe's name to sell tickets. One sports writer keenly observed at the time:

One might have thought that baseball was a sufficient drawing card in itself, but Manager McGraw's reported decision to sign Jim Thorpe, the famous Indian athlete . . . without knowing anything about his ability as a player, arouses the suspicion that it is "anything to get money" in baseball, same as in pretty much anything else. Thorpe, on account of his international prominence . . . would indeed be a drawing card for some, even if he only strolled back and forth in front of the grandstand.[47]

This observation turned out to be prophetic. McGraw used Thorpe's name to ensure large crowds of spectators but told Thorpe that he was a rookie who must work his way up from the bottom like everyone else. So Thorpe found himself spending most of the season on the bench. This was not the only thing that disappointed Thorpe about his first professional position. He himself was calm, easy-going, and thoroughly likable—in the words of one of his Giants teammates, "just like a big overgrown kid." McGraw, on the other hand, was blunt, strict, domineering, and largely humorless. This clash of personalities often resulted in arguments between the two men. All this was extremely frustrating for Thorpe, who only wanted to enjoy playing the game. Rookie or not, he knew that he was a skilled competitor, and he proved it on those few occasions when McGraw allowed him to play. Al Schacht, a Giants pitcher who became Thorpe's friend, later stated:

In my opinion, for a fellow that never played much baseball before, he was a hell of a ballplayer. He could hit the ball as far as anybody and he was one of the fastest men I ever saw running the bases. He played the outfield, mostly right field, and he was good at that, too. He had a great arm.[48]

A Wife and Son

Luckily for Thorpe, at the time he had a pleasant home life that distracted him from and helped him cope with his job-related frustrations. He and Iva had

The 1915 Giants baseball team stands in its batting order, with Thorpe third from the rear.

Thorpe's wedding party. He stands seventh from the left and Iva sits in front of him.

married in October 1913 and rented an apartment in New York City near the Polo Grounds, the stadium where the Giants played their home games. Her gentle nature, thoughtfulness, and companionship added a large measure of comfort and stability to his life. She traveled with him when the Giants played in other cities, and the young couple enjoyed the off-the-field aspects of these trips. They had the opportunity to see many parts of the country and to stay at comfortable hotels. They also ate at restaurants often, both at home and on the road, a luxury they could afford on his considerable salary. Thorpe loved to eat, and the sheer size of his meals regularly raised eyebrows. Describing one of his typical hotel breakfasts, one of his teammates recalled:

> Jim would blow into the dining room about 10 and immediately be surrounded by waiters. He would always begin by saying he wasn't very hungry. This is what usually followed: grapefruit, cereal, half a dozen eggs with

ham, sirloin steak with onions, fried potatoes, sausages, rolls, a pot of coffee.[49]

Like the other people close to Thorpe, Iva could see that he was not happy playing for the Giants. She watched with increasing concern as his run-ins with McGraw became more frequent. In the manager's eyes, one of Thorpe's worst offenses was his tendency to get into informal wrestling matches with the other players. Almost always, it was the players who challenged or provoked him into these bouts. Thorpe was just trying to have a good time, but McGraw felt such behavior was bad for team morale. Thorpe recorded one particularly memorable incident in his scrapbook, saying:

> We were shagging flies [catching balls] in the outfield before a game, and Jeff Tesreau, who was a pretty good pitcher, began scuffling around with me. Finally, I pinned him with an arm lock. The next day McGraw wanted him to pitch and Jeff said he couldn't because he had a sore arm but Jeff wouldn't

Problems with Baseball

Al Schacht, a baseball player for the New York Giants, observed the problems Thorpe encountered on the team, including his personality clash with manager John McGraw and his lack of experience in the game. Robert W. Wheeler quotes Schacht's recollection in Jim Thorpe: World's Greatest Athlete.

"Jim was a fantastic guy. He had a terrific personal appeal to people and was just like a big overgrown kid, in the same mold as Babe Ruth. McGraw had just the opposite type of personality, and the two clashed time and time again. He was a very strict manager. . . . McGraw always wanted to think for the members of his team. He would take all of the responsibilities. He ran the ball game. You could make all the errors in the world, but if you pulled a bum play or if he thought you weren't hustling, he would call you everything. He would get on you and tear you apart, no matter how important you were. He was all order and was the boss at all times. . . . Now as soon as Jim Thorpe came to the Giants, the pressure was on him. It would have been unbearable for anyone else. Here he was, the greatest athlete of all times. . . . For all-around ability as a trackman or as a football player, no one else excelled in so many different departments. But when it came to baseball, he had virtually no experience and was faced with the very best of pitching as soon as he started. You just can't do that! He was a football player, first, and an athlete in everything else, except baseball. He was originally signed only because his name was Jim Thorpe but, after that first year, he stayed in the big leagues on his own."

Thorpe in his Giants uniform in 1917.

Thorpe proudly holds his son, Jim Jr., in 1915.

ropes of various sports as he grew older. But in 1918 the boy contracted a serious illness, possibly influenza, and died. Thorpe was crushed. Al Schacht later remembered:

I will never forget seeing Jim together with his little boy. It was during the spring training of 1917 and they were there with Mrs. Thorpe, who was a very beautiful woman. After practice, they would all be out on the front lawn, in front of the hotel, and the kid would climb up one of Jim's arms and down the other and would grin that great big wide grin just like his old man and the two of them would laugh. After his death, Jim was never the same.[51]

After the tragedy, Thorpe's job with the Giants ended fairly quickly. He often became sullen and touchy, even around his teammates, and the major blow-up with McGraw, which everyone said was long overdue, eventually occurred. According to Al Schacht, who witnessed the event:

Jim missed a signal while running the bases and it cost a run. McGraw was furious and called Jim a "dumb Indian." This was the only thing that Jim would not tolerate and he took out after McGraw and chased him all over the Polo Grounds. It took half the team to stop him. When Jim was dismissed, McGraw used the excuse of his inability to hit a curve ball and the writers have echoed his [inaccurate] statement ever since.[52]

squawk, so McGraw said, "You don't have to tell me. I saw you wrestling with that big Indian yesterday. I'll have no more of that on this ball club." He called me in and threatened to fine me if I roughhoused any of the other players, and I said that was all right with me, because I didn't want to roughhouse with them anyway, but they were always challenging me.[50]

Thorpe's attitude toward McGraw, and in fact toward life in general, turned more bitter after tragedy once more struck him. In 1915 he and Iva had had a son, whom they named James Jr., and the boy immediately became one of the bright spots of Thorpe's life. Everyone remarked how much James Jr. looked like his father, and Thorpe dreamed of teaching him the

Thorpe spent the next few years playing on a variety of baseball teams and did well. For example, in 1920, playing in the International League, he batted an impressive .360, stole twenty-two bases, and hit sixteen home runs. But for him baseball was not enough. He wanted to devote more of his time to football, which, largely because of him, was finally taking off as a professional sport.

Professional Football

Thorpe had begun playing pro football on a part-time basis in 1915. At the time, most sports promoters felt that few people would pay to see football, so only a few small pro teams existed in the country. Jack Cusack, owner of one of these teams, the Canton (Ohio) Bulldogs, believed in the future of the game. He was sure that if he could sign up someone with the drawing power of Jim Thorpe, he could prove football was profitable. Risking bankruptcy, Cusack offered Thorpe what was then an immense sum for playing football—$250 per game. Thorpe reasoned that he could easily squeeze in a few football games in the fall when he was not involved in baseball. He accepted the offer and, sure enough, the crowds began to show up.

In the next few years, thanks to Cusack's increasing success, other pro football teams sprang up, and the game became more and more popular. Some of these teams were able to attract talented former college players like Thorpe. He soon found himself playing with or

A Rough-and-Tumble Game

Most of the colorful early pro football teams no longer exist. Among them was the Canton Bulldogs, owned by Jack Cusack, for whom Jim Thorpe played. In this firsthand account, quoted in Robert W. Wheeler's Jim Thorpe: World's Greatest Athlete, *Cusack recalls one of the Bulldogs' tougher games.*

"Our next opponent, on October 30 [1916], was the burly Columbus Panhandles, long rated as the toughest team in Ohio, but even this formidable aggregation [group] found the Canton defense too strong. At times, Captain Ted Nesser, one of the five brothers who played for Columbus through the entire battle, managed to pierce Canton's first defense line, but he never got past fullback Carp Julian. It was in this game that Captain Ted's redoubtable [awesome] brother, Frank, met a superior in punting when he competed with Canton's Thorpe. The Indian got all of his kicks away in beautiful style and on one occasion lifted the ball down the field for eighty-five yards, booting from his own 15-yard line over the Panhandle goal. It was a rough-and-tumble game filled with penalties, but the Bulldogs, playing it carefully, gave the Panhandles their first defeat of the season, 12–0."

against some of his old Carlisle buddies, including Gus Welch and Pete Calac. But Thorpe remained the game's model player and its biggest draw. Cusack later cited one of Canton's 1917 battles as a typical example of how Thorpe dominated every game he played:

> A striking example of Bulldog power was given the 6,000 fans right from the start. Opening up on their own 23-yard line, Big Jim Thorpe and his eager helpers marched the ball down the field for seventy-seven yards without hesitating. It took just four minutes to travel the distance and send Thorpe across for a touchdown.[53]

By 1920, pro football had become so popular that many managers felt it was

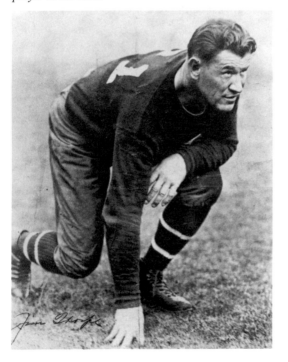

Thorpe as a Canton Bulldog, circa 1919. He received $250 per game, far more than any other player at the time.

time to begin forming leagues like the ones in baseball. Leagues would help make pro football more credible and official in the sports world by organizing and regulating the game. On September 17, 1920, representatives of eleven teams met in an automobile showroom in Canton. They established the American Professional Football Association, or APFA, which eventually would be renamed the National Football League, or NFL. There was no argument about whose name would be used to promote the new league. Everyone voted to make Jim Thorpe the organization's first president, at the time a nonpaying job. Thorpe had few actual duties and acted mainly as a figurehead, his fame making the league look more prestigious.

Even after the formation of the APFA, Thorpe continued to play baseball in the spring and football in the fall. He was constantly on the move, traveling from city to city and spending almost all his time either playing, practicing, or socializing with his teammates. This left little time for his home life. By 1923, Iva had had enough of it and divorced him. Their breakup may have been inevitable anyway, for they had been steadily drifting apart since the death of their son. They had produced three daughters—Gail, Charlotte, and Grace—since that time, but with his busy schedule, Thorpe was unable to spend much time with them. That only drove him and Iva farther apart.

The Game Winds Down

Two years after the divorce, in October 1925, he married an Ohio woman named Freeda Kirkpatrick. She bore him four

A Running Oak Tree

In this anecdote, quoted by Robert W. Wheeler in Jim Thorpe: World's Greatest Athlete, *Canton Bulldog Carp Julian remembers Jim Thorpe's enormous power as a ball carrier.*

"You'd dive at him and hit him and after a time, when you came to, you'd wonder if the roof had fallen in. He'd run down the field and in his wake you'd see a string of prostrate [flattened] football players. He seemed to run with his knees up to his chin, and no one wanted any of that. If you went for him from the side, he'd bump you into next week with the swerve of a hip. He was like an oak tree doing a hundred yards in 10 seconds."

sons—Carl Philip, William, Richard, and John—in quick succession. At first, despite his hectic schedule, the new family was fairly happy. Perhaps this was because Thorpe was overjoyed at having sons and made an extra effort to spend time with them.

Spending this extra time was easier than it had been before because Thorpe's career was winding down. He realized that he was getting steadily older, slower, and less agile and that he would have to quit professional sports soon. Nevertheless, even the aging, less effective Jim Thorpe was a faster, stronger, and more formidable football player than most of the men in the league. Carp Julian, one of his Canton teammates, recalled:

Late in his career, he encountered an opposing tackle who played dirty and ignored Jim's slow motion warnings to stop it. The next time he tried a dirty trick, Jim stopped dead, put the ball down and looked at the tackle. The tackle dived for the ball. He picked it up. That put the shoe on the other foot. Jim tackled him so hard it shook the earth. "You must not do that to Jim," Thorpe admonished [lectured]. But the tackle never heard. He was out cold.[54]

Despite his considerable abilities, however, Thorpe knew when it was time to quit. He played his final pro baseball game in 1928 and his last pro football game in 1929, when he was forty-one. Pro football would, thanks to his tireless efforts, go on to become bigger and more popular than ever. But at the time, most players sensed that for them, without Jim Thorpe, the game would never again be quite the same.

6 The Drifter

The next two decades were difficult for Jim Thorpe. Despite his worldwide fame and many memorable accomplishments, he found it difficult to make a living outside the pro sports world. He drifted across the country from one low-paying job to another in order to support his family. To his dismay, many of his employers did not care who he had been on the playing fields or that he had once brought the country honor and glory in the Olympics. So they thought nothing of paying him substandard wages or even trying to cheat him. As if trying to claim some of his past dignity, during this difficult period Thorpe petitioned the AAU to regain his amateur status. But, as would be the case in many later such attempts, the organization flatly refused his request. Occasional bright spots did illuminate these lean years. From time to time, Thorpe landed jobs playing Indians in Hollywood films or enjoyed the attention when individuals and groups recognized and paid tribute to him. But these occasions were the exception rather than the rule. Most of the time, the great athlete who had once been the focus of cheering crowds and the world press found himself largely ignored or forgotten.

Thorpe plays with his sons, Carl Philip (left) and Billy, about 1931.

Thinking of the Days That Were

Late in 1929, after retiring from pro football, Jim Thorpe was filled with optimism. He was sure that he could do just as well outside the sports world as he had within it. But several factors worked against his achieving this goal. For one thing, in the same year he chose to retire from sports the stock market crashed and the country, as well as the rest of the world, sank into economic depression. Jobs of any kind were scarce, and well-paying work was almost nonexistent. Also, Thorpe had few skills beyond his athletic abilities. He knew a little about carpentry and tailoring, which he had picked up years before at Carlisle. But he lacked the background to land a lucrative professional position, such as banker or company manager. In addition, he knew little about how much he should be paid, which made it easy for employers to take advantage of him. And he also generously but unwisely gave to needy friends much of the little money he did make. As a result, it was difficult for him to save and easy for others to take advantage of him.

And Thorpe found himself taken advantage of almost the moment he left sports. He received word that MGM Studios in Hollywood was interested in buying the rights to his life story for a film titled *Red Son of Carlisle*. He had been thinking about trying his hand at film acting anyway, so he moved to California to be near Hollywood. Not realizing the great value of the rights to his story, Thorpe sold them for a mere $1,500, perhaps one-tenth or less of their worth at the time. And the film was never made. Not surprisingly, the money did not last long and while waiting for movie work to open up he took a job as a judge at a cheap California dance marathon. At the time these contests in which couples competed for money and prizes by seeing who could continue dancing the longest were a national fad. Sportswriter Art Cohn happened to see Thorpe at the marathon and afterward wrote:

> There he was—a powerful giant, 210 pounds of All-Time All-American— watching the shuffling feet of several worn and weary couples as they fought themselves through the dance marathon. For Jim Thorpe, you know, is referee of this latest madness [silly fad]! . . . For the most part, he sits alone in a sequestered [secluded] corner of the big tent. Perhaps thinking of the days that were—when he booted four field goals against Harvard, when he won highest laurels at the 1912 Olympics, when Walter Camp made him All-American—and when he was stripped of his honors. Pleasant memories and bitter ones. He is like a restless pilgrim, never remaining long in any one place.[55]

Too Big a Heart

Indeed, Thorpe continued to drift, taking one job after another, always hoping that the next one would be better than the last. Early in 1930, after officiating at several other dance marathons, he signed on as a painter for a Los Angeles oil company. For several months he painted gas stations and oil trucks and, to his surprise, found that some of his fellow workers had never heard of him. In October he managed to get a small role as Chief Black Crow in a movie. Bit parts in two more films followed. Then, desperate for money, he accepted a four-dollar-a-day job digging the excavation for the new Los Angeles County Hospital. Again, a newspaper man—this one a reporter for the *New York Times*—spotted him. Amazed that Thorpe, so obviously down on his luck, was still able to smile, the reporter wrote:

> "I'm not through," he [Thorpe] said today. Jim is a non-entity [unknown person] in a motley crew of diggers. . . . After work Jim goes home to a very small cottage where Mrs. Thorpe, who also can smile, and [Carl] Philip, 4, and Billy, 2, wait for him. Sometimes at night Jim opens a big book [his personal scrapbook] and the little Thorpes are properly awed, as though understanding it all. The book contains many clippings and some pho-

tographs. . . . It's hard to find a reason for the present state of affairs of the smiling former athletic hero. "Guess it's an old story," he grins. "I liked to be a good fellow with the boys [lending his friends money]. But I'll come out of this, and I'll do some saving when I do."[56]

But in the following years Thorpe was unable to save any substantial sum. This was partly because it was expensive to support a wife and four sons, but also because he so often agreed to give his time free of charge. For instance, beginning in the mid-1930s, he made frequent speeches to schools, clubs, and charity functions. He thought it was wrong to take money for these engagements and even ended up paying from his own pocket for the travel expenses involved. Remembering Thorpe's unusual generosity, restaurant owner and friend Slim Harrison remarked:

Thorpe takes a break from his job digging the excavation for the L.A. County Hospital in 1931.

Thorpe, wearing his Native American costume, poses with Olympic swimmer Josephine McKim shortly before the 1932 Los Angeles games.

I had the pleasure and honor of knowing Jim Thorpe and associating with him for the last twenty years of his life. In my opinion, the only fault he had was that his heart was too big for him. He never failed to accommodate a friend. Any money-raising charitable event that came along, if a request went to Jim to put in an appearance, he was never too busy. He would devote his time to that and he enjoyed it.[57]

Trying to keep up his charitable endeavors and still make ends meet, Thorpe continued to take whatever menial jobs he could find. Sometimes he found it difficult to keep his spirits up and remain optimistic about the future.

A Few Uplifting Moments

Amidst the hard times, however, Thorpe enjoyed a few bright and uplifting moments. The first of these was at the 1932 Olympic Games, which were held in Los Angeles not far from where he was living. He wanted to attend, of course, but found that he could not afford to buy tickets for himself and his family. When the press got wind of this, people from across the country wrote to Thorpe offering to pay for the tickets. On the opening day of the games, Charles Curtis, vice president of the United States and also a Native American, asked him to sit beside him. And when Thorpe sat down, the audience of 105,000 people gave him a standing ovation.

Later in the 1930s, Thorpe's hopes were briefly raised when it appeared that his movie career might finally take off. He landed supporting roles in *She, The Green Light, You Can't Take It with You*, and several westerns. While on the set of one frontier epic, Thorpe good-naturedly allowed some of the actors to use him in playing some practical jokes. Authors Frank Scully and Norman Sper later reported in *American Mercury* magazine:

Some college athletes were in the picture and they were jumping around between takes, placing bets on their skill in the standing broad jump. They got up to ten feet. Bill Frawley [who later played Fred Mertz in TV's "I Love Lucy"], an actor, learned from the director that the stage Indian was Jim Thorpe. Frawley decided to cook up a surprise. He told the crowd that he had an old man of 50 who he thought could beat the college athletes. Bets climbed until Frawley had to cover a pool of $100 before the books closed. Jim took off his feathers, left on the moccasins. He flexed his leg muscles three times and jumped—10 feet 8 inches. That's only six inches behind the world's record.[58]

Thorpe, in costume, stands behind actor Randolph Scott on the set of the movie She *in 1935.*

Another activity that Thorpe took pride in during the 1930s was his work championing the plight of his fellow Indians. He, like many other Native Americans, believed that it was time for the U.S. government to stop regulating the lives of most Indians on reservations. As had been the case for decades, a government agency known as the Bureau of Indian Affairs ran the reservations across the country and made most of the important decisions about the rights, privileges, and futures of most Native Americans. The government also had laws allowing officials in Washington, D.C., to control Native American property. Because of these restrictions, most American Indians did not enjoy the benefits of full U.S. citizenship. Thorpe wanted the government to eliminate the Bureau of Indian Affairs and repeal the property laws. In 1937 he lobbied for these aims on behalf of the Sac and Fox tribe, saying:

> There hasn't been a single poor Indian helped by any of this legislation. The Indian who has the money is the Indian the government is always wanting to protect. We are trying to keep our tribe free from government meddling, to give the Indian a chance to stand on his own.[59]

Thorpe used his name to help support passage of the Wheeler Bill, which would have repealed much former Indian-related legislation and set up local tribal corporations to handle Indian affairs. But the House of Representatives killed the bill by a vote of 202 to 120. Thorpe remarked unhappily that this returned the Indian "to the blanket," or to subservient status, but he remained proud of his lobbying effort and thereafter helped Native American causes whenever possible.

Pushing for Indian Independence

In his lobbying for Native American rights in the late 1930s, Jim Thorpe maintained that Indians should be considered on an equal basis with other citizens. This statement is quoted from his personal scrapbook (printed in Robert W. Wheeler's Jim Thorpe: World's Greatest Athlete*).*

"The Indian should be permitted to grow out of his tribal bonds into representative American citizenship. He should not be forced into communistic cooperatives [contained communities] fostered under the Thomas-Rogers Act [a bill designed to closely regulate Indian reservations]. Instead, the 6,000 [whites] now employed in political jobs administering Indian affairs should be dismissed and the Indians should begin management of their own business. Governmental paternalism [providing for people without giving them any responsibility] has failed in all aspects. . . . The administrators, all the way from John Collier, commissioner of Indian Affairs, to agents and reservation superintendents, have built up a perpetual guardianship. The Indian should be permitted to shed his inferiority complex and live like a normal American citizen."

Relentless Travel Takes Its Toll

By 1940 it was clear that Thorpe's movie career was never to be. The best he could hope for in Hollywood, agents told him, was an occasional bit part as an Indian or has-been football player. So he continued to busy himself with whatever work he could find. He managed to become involved with a lecture-booking organization, the W. Colston Leigh Bureau, which offered him a nationwide tour. This time Thorpe made money for his lectures, although not nearly as much as he needed. Choosing to appear in traditional Indian attire, he spoke before school assemblies and other groups on subjects ranging from his own famous sports feats to Indian culture. Eventually, he was doing as many as four lectures a week and constantly traveling. In one lecture that he repeated often, he stated proudly:

I came from the Sac and Fox tribe in Oklahoma, and I have never forgotten that I am an Indian. No Indian can forget it. Indians, you know, are misnamed. We aren't Indians. We are Red Men and we settled this country long before the white people ever came to these shores. Why then should we be deprived of our citizenship until we can qualify through a written examination? None of you here is a government ward. You are citizens because that heritage has been passed on to you. But Red Men are wards of the government. There were 30,000 Indian volunteers in the last war [World War I]. They fought for this country. Many gave their lives for its people and its resources. In return, the Indians should be granted full citizenship, with all the rights and privileges that go with it. . . . I would like to ask every one of you here to work for the improvement of Indian conditions. They can be bettered with your help. Perhaps some day another Abraham Lincoln will come along to free the Red Men of this country.[60]

After a while, Thorpe's characteristic relentless schedule affected his marriage to Freeda, just as it had doomed his relationship with Iva. Freeda had stayed with

Thorpe advocates citizenship for American Indians at a Vallejo, California, night club.

him for years as he scratched for a living. But now she had also to bear his being away for long periods, sometimes without a single word or letter. Despite her efforts to accept the situation, the couple grew apart, and Freeda filed for divorce in April 1941. Thorpe's daughter Grace later explained the breakup, remembering how

> Dad used to take off for two or three weeks. She wouldn't know where he was. Nothing. He did the same thing with my mother [Iva]. It goes back to the old days when the [Indian] men used to do that. They would go off and hunt buffalo. That was just the Indian way of doing it. White women don't understand.[61]

For Thorpe, the divorce, which he did not expect or want, was one more tragedy to deal with and he had to fight to keep from sinking into depression. "I cannot decide," he commented at the time, "whether I was well named or not. Many a time the path has gleamed bright for me, but just as often it has been dark and bitter indeed."[62]

His Patriotic Duty

Whether bright or dark, Thorpe's path continued to zigzag. After the United States entered World War II late in 1941, he felt it his patriotic duty to help in the war effort. Far too old to enter the service, he took a job in a Dearborn, Michigan, plant that produced military vehicles. There, in 1943, at the age of fifty-five, he suffered a serious heart attack. The news got out and letters poured in from around the country. One fifteen-year-old boy from Raleigh, North Carolina, wrote, "Knute

Facing and Defeating Death

After his 1943 heart attack, Thorpe received many get-well letters. One of his favorites, quoted here from Jim Thorpe: World's Greatest Athlete, *by Robert W. Wheeler, was this note from Ben Templeton of Raleigh, North Carolina.*

"Dear Mr. Thorpe: I was eating supper tonight when over the radio Bill Stern [an announcer] said something about America's greatest athlete. I knew right away he was talking about you. He said this athlete was sick. Then he said it was you. He said you had a heart attack. I went right to my desk and started writing you this letter. Mr. Thorpe, he said that Knute Rockne once said that you couldn't be stopped, but that now you were almost stopped. You can't die, Mr. Thorpe! You will always live in my memory. I have never seen you perform, but I have heard so much about you that I have begun to like you very much. I am only a boy of 15, but I like sports, and I like to play them. As one sports lover to another, please, Mr. Thorpe get well. If you get well, sports will mean more to me and millions of other American boys like me to know that a true sportsman can pull through anything, that they have guts enough to face death in the face and defeat death. So, Mr. Thorpe, please, please get well soon.

P.S. I know that you have never heard of me and don't know me, but I know you are the greatest sportsman that ever lived."

Rockne [a famous football coach] once said that you couldn't be stopped. . . . You can't die, Mr. Thorpe! You will always live in my memory."[63]

Recovering from his illness, Thorpe realized that he had been pushing himself much too hard, that to survive he must try to slow down. He returned to Oklahoma, where, with Freeda's consent, he enrolled their sons in a local Indian school similar to the ones he had attended as a boy. Though he himself had hated school, he had learned how important education was and wanted to set his children on the path of learning. Thorpe now resumed his lectures, but this time on a less hectic schedule.

In 1945 Thorpe's life took still another unexpected turn when he married for the third time. His new bride, Patricia Askew, a native of Louisville, Kentucky, had been an admirer of his since his pro football days. She was a smart and well-organized businesswoman and immediately took charge of his financial affairs. She made sure that he received larger fees for his speaking engagements and that the family bills were

Kicking and Catching a Punt

In some of the many lectures he delivered to school children, Thorpe described the proper technique in various football plays. In this excerpt, quoted in Robert W. Wheeler's Jim Thorpe: World's Greatest Athlete, *Thorpe discusses punting.*

"In order to punt the spiral with accuracy, the ball should be held as far away from the body as possible, directly in front of the kicking foot, with one hand on each side of it and the outer point of the ball slightly lower than the end nearest the body. At the same time, taking a short step with the other foot, drop the ball so that it falls without turning and meet it with the instep of the kicking foot about two and one-half feet from the ground. The foot should be extended and the leg should swing mostly from the hip and but little at the knee. The punt should be followed through with the leg as far as possible with the body bent backward so as to get the full weight into the kick. An important fact to remember in catching punts is to watch the ball every instant and be in the proper position to receive it by seeing the direction toward which its lower end is pointing while descending. When the spiral descends with its forward end nearest the ground, the ball will carry much further than it will when it descends with its back end inclined downward."

Thorpe offers pointers to boys cast as sandlot ballplayers in the film The Life of Knute Rockne.

Jim and Patricia Thorpe read fan letters in 1952.

paid on time. This took a great deal of pressure off Thorpe and helped him enjoy life more than he had in a long time.

Patricia was surprised but not upset when Thorpe unexpectedly joined the U.S. Merchant Marine in the summer of 1945. He wanted one last chance to serve his country and worked as a ship's carpenter on the U.S.S. *Southwest Victory* for about two months. When he returned home, Patricia helped him get back into a leisurely, but reasonably well-paying lecture schedule.

For the next three years, Thorpe supplemented his public speaking by occasionally teaching children the fundamentals of track and field in park recreation programs. As he had, with only occasional exceptions during the past two decades, he remained out of the national spotlight. But this was about to change. For Jim Thorpe, 1949 would mark the beginning of a new era, one in which he and an enthusiastic press and public would revisit and honor his past glories.

7 The Legend

Beginning in 1949, Jim Thorpe enjoyed a sudden resurgence of public interest in himself and his athletic accomplishments. As the midpoint of the twentieth century neared, sportswriters and enthusiasts scurried to compile lists of the greatest sports figures of the past fifty years. Inevitably, Thorpe's name appeared on every list. Hollywood was quick to take advantage of the renewed interest in past sports heroes and planned a number of related film biographies. One of these was Thorpe's own story, which was to make it to the screen at last. The publicity surrounding the sports lists and the movie, in turn, sparked new concerns for his lost medals, and friends petitioned the AAU once again on his behalf. All these activities served to thrust Thorpe back into the national spotlight. Filled with joy and pride over all this attention and recognition, he would remain in that spotlight, an undeniable legend in his own time, until his death.

Public Attention Increases

Thorpe got his first inkling of the coming resurgence of interest in him late in 1948. He noticed that the offers to make public appearances and work with young athletes

were steadily increasing. Late in September, for example, the coach of the Israel National Soccer Team asked him to help prepare his players for their upcoming match against the U.S. team at the Polo Grounds in New York City. "I deem it an honor," remarked the coach, "to appoint

Thorpe and Haim Glovinsky, president of the Israel Football Association, in 1948.

America's greatest athlete to train our team."[64] Later, at the game itself, Thorpe, now sixty years old, gave a football-kicking exhibition during half-time. He amazed the spectators by unleashing a punt of more than seventy-five yards, farther than many college athletes at the time could kick.

The number of invitations Thorpe received to attend sports awards dinners also increased. A few months after his New York kicking display, he appeared at the National Sports Awards Dinner in Los Angeles. Reporters and athletes crowded around him, eager to shake his hand and ask him about his legendary deeds. There, Thorpe met seventeen-year-old Bob Mathias, who had won the Olympic Decathlon in the 1948 Olympics. *Los Angeles Times* sportswriter Jack Geyer recorded this historic meeting between two great Olympic champions:

> I intercepted Thorpe on the way to his table and asked if he'd mind posing for a picture with Mathias. "I'd like to meet that boy," Jim said, so we started for Bob's table. Bob saw Thorpe coming, got up and ran toward him with his hand outstretched. "I'm glad to know you, Mr. Thorpe. I've heard so much about you," Bob said. "I've heard a lot about you too," Jim answered. Then they shook hands and just beamed at each other for several seconds without saying anything.[65]

As more and more sportswriters began recalling Thorpe's past triumphs, Hollywood took notice. It appeared certain that Thorpe's name would appear on the Associated Press's list of the half-century's greatest football players, slated to be released in 1950. Warner Brothers Studio,

eager to cash in on this free publicity, wanted to start production on a Thorpe film as soon as possible. Warners bought the rights from MGM early in 1949 and in August announced that work was beginning on the film, to be titled *Jim Thorpe—All American*. Thorpe was delighted at this turn of events. He was even more thrilled when the studio asked him to be the technical adviser for the project. In the following months, he periodically visited the set, offering the writers and director information and stories about situations in his life. He also worked with Burt Lancaster, cast in the lead role, teaching the movie star how players had kicked and handled the football in the early days of the pro sport.

Actor Burt Lancaster as the great athlete in the 1951 film Jim Thorpe—All American. *Lancaster, a talented athlete himself, did most of his own stunts in this and other films.*

An Actor Trains

In this excerpt, quoted by Robert W. Wheeler in Jim Thorpe: World's Greatest Athlete, *actor Burt Lancaster recalls his physical training for playing Thorpe in the film biography and his memory of Thorpe himself at the time.*

"I remember at one football practice during the making of the film, Thorpe, who was sitting in the stands watching us, came over and showed me how to kick the ball. He said some very kind things like, 'That's fine. You are doing it well.' He was a bear of a man, somewhere around sixty or thereabouts. I wasn't a kid myself either. I was thirty-seven when I did the picture and had to go into a lot of serious training. You know, I had to learn to play football, and toward the end we had a seventeen-day period in which I worked out with all the football players from USC and UCLA. By the end of that time I could actually stay in there and maneuver. I had to learn how to high jump a certain way and learn how to put the shot, the discus, and all those things. Jess Hill, the former athletic director at USC, who was at the time the track coach, trained me along with a boy called Al Lawrence, who doubled me [on film in difficult stunts] and later finished third in the American Decathlon. I was in really wonderful condition in those days. I did roadwork [running] every single day for three solid weeks. I learned to run, learned to hurdle, not that I was particularly good, but I mean I was able to put the shot, the discus, and the javelin very well, that is, with form. You know, we could trick the distances. All I had to do was to look pretty good doing it, you see, and then of course the problem was the acting. The first thing they did was dye my hair black."

A publicity photo of Lancaster as Thorpe.

Thorpe in 1950 with Babe Didrikson, Associated Press's choice as the greatest female athlete of the first half of the century.

Topping the Lists

As the shooting of the film continued into 1950, Thorpe found himself the recipient of a seemingly never-ending shower of honors. Sure enough, as many people had expected, his name was on the Associated Press's list of great football players, published on January 24, 1950. But to Thorpe's surprise, he was not merely *on* the list. He was at the top! Of the 391 prominent sportswriters and broadcasters polled, 170 had voted Thorpe the greatest football player of the first half of the century. Harold "Red" Grange had come in second with 138 votes, and Bronko Nagurski had scored 38 votes for third place. No other nominee had received more than a half-dozen votes.

Thorpe's name and accomplishments were already appearing daily in newspapers across the country when, just a little over two weeks later, he received an even greater honor. On February 11, 1950, the Associated Press announced the results of its poll of the best all-around male athletes of the first half of the century. Thorpe's name again topped the list, this time by an even greater margin. According to sportswriter Gayle Talbot:

> Jim Thorpe, that almost legendary figure of the sports world, had additional laurels heaped upon his leathern [aging] brow today when the nation's sports experts named him the greatest male athlete of the half-century. Previously voted the No. 1 football player of the past 50 years, the wonderful Sac and Fox became the only double winner in the Associated Press poll when 252 out of 393 sports writers and radio broadcasters accorded him the ultimate honor.[66]

Baseball legend Babe Ruth was second in the poll, receiving eighty-six votes, and champion boxer Jack Dempsey came in third with nineteen votes.

Further tributes and honors followed. Press organizations in several other countries also sponsored polls of the century's greatest athletes. And in poll after poll, Thorpe's name topped the lists. *El Universal*, a Venezuelan newspaper, for example, announced that South Americans had picked Thorpe number one over Babe Ruth, track star Jesse Owens, and boxers Jack Dempsey and Joe Louis. As a result of these honors, Thorpe was suddenly an international celebrity. As Gregory Richards put it:

> Hundreds of groups requested appearances by Thorpe. He was invited to a great many honorary banquets, was given the key to the city of Philadelphia, and was welcomed back to Carlisle and Canton for various celebrations. Thorpe was also entered in the National College Football Hall of Fame.[67]

Among the Carlisle tributes was the dedication of a stone monument at the school in a ceremony Thorpe himself attended. There were tears in his eyes as he witnessed the unveiling of the tablet, on which appeared the words: "In recognition of the athletic achievements of Jim Thorpe, student of the Carlisle Indian School, Olympic champion at Stockholm in 1912, and in 1950 voted the greatest athlete and football player of the first half of the 20th century."

The Saga of Chief Bright Path

During the long string of tributes to Thorpe, the topic of the loss of his Olympic medals inevitably resurfaced. On several past occasions, the most recent in 1948, various individuals and organizations had requested that the AAU and U.S.

Dedication of the stone monument in Carlisle in 1951. Thorpe (second from left) is flanked by his son, Carl Philip, and Phyllis Thaxter, who played Mrs. Thorpe in the movie.

Thorpe, aged sixty-three, attends the premiere of Jim Thorpe—All American *in August 1951.*

Olympic Committee reinstate Thorpe and return his prizes. All these attempts had been in vain. Now, prompted by Thorpe's friends and by growing popular sentiment, four U.S. congressmen made still another attempt on the great athlete's behalf. One of the legislators commented, "Restoration [of the medals] would right the wrong done to Thorpe and would give recognition to him and to the American Indians." [68] But to everyone's dismay, AAU and Olympic Committee officials, for reasons unknown, refused to budge from their position. Thorpe would not be reinstated.

Thorpe was sorely disappointed but decided that the refusal was a minor setback in an otherwise exciting and happy period. Indeed, only a few months later there was more cause for celebration. On August 23, 1951, Warner Brothers released the long-awaited *Jim Thorpe—All American*. The film had a double world premiere, with initial showings in Carlisle, Pennsylvania, and Oklahoma City, a move designed to honor Thorpe. Thorpe, his

son Carl Philip, Phyllis Thaxter, the actress who played one of Thorpe's wives in the film, and the governor of Pennsylvania attended the Carlisle showing. The movie did brisk business at the box office—no surprise, considering how popular Thorpe was at the time. It also generated a considerable number of magazine and newspaper articles. Typical was one titled "Thorpe Film Tells Honest Story," in the *Los Angeles Mirror*, which commented:

> Starring Burt Lancaster as Thorpe and with Charles Bickford looking remarkably like a younger "Pop" Warner than we know today, the film brings to the screen highlights in the saga of Chief Bright Path, a man whose path has at times shined the brightest of all the world's athletes, but which at times has been overcast by shadows of doubt and indecision . . . shadows, too, of charges of professionalism, loss of Olympic Games medals and the bitter tragedy that comes with the death of a first son. [69]

Thorpe receives some of the donations sent from around the country by fans who had heard about his financial troubles.

Some of the articles inspired by the movie told a different kind of story. They drew attention to the sad fact that the man whose phenomenal and heroic deeds had been depicted on the screen was financially nearly destitute. Some writers complained that Thorpe should have shared in the film's considerable profits. "So what does Thorpe get from all this," asked one writer, "from the 50-cent pieces—give or take a couple of nickels—that are tossed through the box office . . . ? The same as you and I, bub. Nothing."[70] Other articles further revealed that Thorpe had developed lip cancer and was entering a Philadelphia hospital for surgery. In a statement that appeared in a number of newspapers around the country, Patricia Thorpe admitted:

We're broke. Jim has nothing but his name and his memories. He has spent money on his own people and has giv-

en it away. He has often been exploited. . . . In desperation, because of lack of funds, Jim and I assembled a bunch of Indians, dancers and singers. We hoped to launch a nationwide night club tour and opened the first engagement several weeks ago in Philadelphia. We have many bookings, but Jim won't be able to fill them in view of what has happened.[71]

An Outpouring of Respect and Affection

Learning of Thorpe's plight, thousands of people offered him help. The surgeon performed the operation for free and donations poured in to help the stricken athlete pay his hospital bill and get back on his feet. Football players at Ohio State

A Daughter Remembers

In this tract, quoted from Gregory Richards' Jim Thorpe: World's Greatest Athlete, *Thorpe's daughter Grace recalls her famous father.*

"As one of Jim Thorpe's daughters from his first marriage to Iva Margaret Miller, I recall my father's sports history by remembering our personal family events. For example, Mother graduated from Carlisle Indian School in Pennsylvania in March of 1912, a few months before Dad won the Decathlon and Pentathlon in the summer Olympics held in Stockholm, Sweden. . . . In 1921, I was born in Yale [Oklahoma] at the Jim Thorpe Home, now a museum operated by the state of Oklahoma Historical Society. . . . Professional football was just getting started in Ohio then and Dad was the first elected president of the American Professional Football Association, now the National Football League. He was in his middle thirties when I was born. I can recall him standing at center field at the Haskell Institute football stadium in Lawrence, Kansas, where I was a five-year-old student. He kicked a football through one goalpost, then turned around and easily kicked another ball to the goalpost at the other end. Unfortunately the glory, fame, and recognition of his athletic accomplishments did not bring him happiness. His personal life was sad, but he learned to overcome tragedy and still perform. . . . In spite of all his personal problems, he was a successful man in his field. He was not a businessman and never learned how to exploit his fame. However, businessmen were in awe of him because they didn't know how to be athletes either."

Thorpe and daughter Grace.

University raised $1,200 and a group of Dallas, Texas, residents sent in more than $500 after hearing a radio announcer mention Thorpe's situation. Donations also came from many Native Americans, high school and college students, and men and women from every branch of the service. One soldier stationed in North Korea wrote:

> I never saw Jim Thorpe, but I've read a lot about him. We don't have any dollar bills out here, but enclosed is my lucky 50-cent piece which I've carried for years. Hope it brings Jim the luck it has brought me.[72]

Thorpe was overwhelmed and touched by this huge outpouring of respect and affection, mostly by people he had never met. He quickly recovered from the surgery and, to the relief of family, friends, and fans alike, seemed to be his old self again.

But only months later, Thorpe's health took another turn for the worse. Late in 1952 he suffered a second heart attack and had to be hospitalized once more. He had not fully recovered from this episode, when, seven months later, he had a third heart attack. On March 28, 1953, Thorpe and Patricia were eating dinner in their Lomita, California, trailer, when he suddenly collapsed. The *New York Times* reported:

> Mrs. Thorpe's screams attracted a neighbor, Cathy Bradshaw, who administered artificial respiration for nearly half an hour. A county fire rescue squad took over and was momentarily successful. Thorpe revived, recognized persons around him and spoke to them. He was conscious for only a brief time before he suffered a relapse and died.[73]

The news of Jim Thorpe's passing brought sorrow to millions of people around the world. Thousands paid their respects, filing past his body as it lay in state for several days after his memorial service. Obituaries in hundreds of newspapers praised Thorpe and his sports accomplishments, while his family received thousands of letters expressing sadness over their loss. It was, many said, also the world's loss. Thorpe's one-time football opponent Dwight Eisenhower, now president of the United States, wrote as follows:

> I learned with sorrow of the death of my old friend, Jim Thorpe. I am delighted that as a tribute to his achievements and to his warm personality, a fitting memorial is to be erected in his memory. Jim has long been recognized as one of the outstanding athletes of our time and has occupied a unique place in the hearts of Americans everywhere. As one who played against him in football more than 40 years ago, I personally feel that no other athlete possessed his all 'round abilities in games and sports.[74]

Many people felt that in a sense, Thorpe had not really died, that he had joined that elite group of persons whose larger-than-life deeds live on in people's memories and hearts. His daughter Grace later summed up this feeling:

> Most famous people are rich. Dad was one of the few who were not. . . . [But] because of his overwhelming success in sports he achieved what few do—he achieved immortality. The name Jim Thorpe will live in the hearts of sports-minded people forever.[75]

The World's Greatest Athlete

After Jim Thorpe's death, his wife Patricia wrestled with the decision of finding a final resting place for her husband. Members of the Sac and Fox tribe wanted him buried in Shawnee, Oklahoma, and offered to erect a fitting memorial. When problems arose in raising the funds for the memorial, however, Patricia looked elsewhere. Eventually, she hit upon the idea of honoring Thorpe's memory by persuading a town to rename itself after him. Newspaper editor Joe Boyle recalled the unlikely story of how Mauch Chunk, a tiny town in eastern Pennsylvania's coal region, came to be known as Jim Thorpe, Pennsylvania:

> I was standing in the National Bank, talking to Gerry Jackson, the cashier, when this woman came in. . . . She introduced herself as Mrs. Jim Thorpe. She had been visiting in Philadelphia when she heard of this unique nickel-a-week plan which we were then developing with the idea of bringing industry to our town. Under this program each resident would contribute five cents a week to the fund. She was impressed by a small town, trying to do a big thing with a little thing—a nickel. Before leaving, Mrs. Thorpe proposed the idea that if we would

consent to change our name to "Jim Thorpe," she would bring Jim's body here, and then the National Fraternal Order of Eagles, of which he had been a member, would create a memorial so that he could be properly edified [remembered]. Then she left. . . . When I spoke to other people in the town, they saw in it a great opportunity to bring the two towns together for the

Patricia Thorpe visits her husband's monument in Jim Thorpe, Pennsylvania. Engraved on it: "Sir, you are the greatest athlete in the world."

first time. Because, actually you see, we had two towns, Mauch Chunk and East Mauch Chunk.[76]

The people of the two towns agreed on the proposed merger and name change, and Patricia Thorpe brought her husband's body to this, its final destination. She placed a different sample of soil at each corner of the monument. One came from the Oklahoma farm where Thorpe grew up. The second was taken from the athletic field at Carlisle and the third from the Polo Grounds in New York, two places where he competed often. The last sample came from the Olympic Stadium in Stockholm, the scene of Thorpe's greatest triumph. The words engraved on his red granite monument read:

"SIR, YOU ARE THE GREATEST ATHLETE IN THE WORLD"

KING GUSTAV STOCKHOLM, SWEDEN
1912 OLYMPICS
1888   JIM THORPE   1953

The town set up summer camps and other youth programs in honor of Thorpe and benefited greatly from the publicity surrounding their new namesake. "We are making more progress now than we ever did before," Joe Boyle remarked. "Jim Thorpe brought these two towns together and gave us our first positive movement in a hundred years."[77] Some of these camps and programs are still in operation. And over the years people from around the country, and also from many foreign countries, have continued to visit the town to pay their respects to the sports hero.

Many other people and groups accorded Jim Thorpe honors in the second half of the century. Soon after his death, the National Football Association began giv-

ing the Jim Thorpe Award, its "most valuable player" trophy. Each year, the most talented player in the game receives the prize in memory of the man who helped make pro football possible. In 1958 the National Indian Hall of Fame in Anadarko, Oklahoma, an institution that honors Native Americans of outstanding achievement, inducted Thorpe. And in 1961 he was elected to the Pennsylvania Hall of Fame. Later such honors included induction into the National Professional Football Hall of Fame and the National Track and Field Hall of Fame.

Despite all these great honors, many people felt that the most significant tribute to Thorpe would be the reinstatement of his status as an amateur and the return of his Olympic medals. Constant pressure by family, friends, and fans finally made the first of these events a reality. On October 13, 1973, the *New York Daily News* reported:

> "Sixty Years Later, Thorpe's Amateur Status Restored." . . . The Amateur Athletic Union Friday restored the amateur standing of fabled Indian athlete Jim Thorpe, who starred in the 1912 Olympics only to be stripped of his gold medals on allegations that he was a professional. The move clears the way for intercession on Thorpe's behalf by the U.S. Olympic Committee with the International Olympic Committee, which stripped Thorpe of his medals in 1913.[78]

But the IOC still refused to return Thorpe's medals. Later, in 1976, Thorpe's daughter Grace approached President Gerald Ford, asking him to see that the IOC discussed the issue again. For reasons unknown, the IOC refused to consider the issue. Grace Thorpe then secured the backing of Senator Alan Cranston of California. He introduced a resolution in the U.S. Congress calling for the IOC to restore Thorpe's medals and records and the resolution passed. But the IOC still would not budge. Finally, in 1982, former treasury secretary William E. Simon, who had recently been elected to head the U.S. Olympic Committee, joined the fight. As Gregory Richards tells it:

> In October of 1982, Simon attended the executive conference of the International Olympic Committee in Lausanne, Switzerland—the city where Thorpe's prizes had been locked up some seventy years before—determined to clear up the Thorpe case. Simon cornered IOC president [Juan Antonio] Samaranch [of Spain] beforehand and bargained with him to bring up the Thorpe matter. Samaranch did bring up the issue and made surprisingly short work of pushing through a decision to restore Thorpe's medals . . . at long last. The many years of frustration had finally come to an end. Just as frustrating, in a sense, was Samaranch's answer as to why it had taken so long for the IOC to clear up the affair: "I don't know. For the first time since I became president we studied this problem, and we solved it in two hours."[79]

In a public ceremony in 1983, the IOC officially honored Thorpe. His records were reentered in the Olympic record books, and each of his seven children received replicas of his gold medals. In the audience were two of Thorpe's children, along with thirteen grandchildren and sixteen great-grandchildren. It was a proud

Thorpe's grandson, Bill Thorpe Jr. (left), carries the Olympic torch at the 1984 Los Angeles games.

and joyous day for all of them, as well as for millions of Thorpe's fans around the world who heard the news through the international media.

Other proud days for Thorpe's family and admirers came the following year. In 1984 the U.S. Postal Service issued a special commemorative stamp honoring Thorpe. And his grandson, Bill Thorpe Jr., was one of the carriers of the Olympic torch at the 1984 Los Angeles Olympics. As they watched the young man proudly carrying the symbol of international competition that day, people around the world were reminded of his famous ancestor. Many paid silent tribute to the modest Native American with the wide grin and the big heart, who will perhaps always be known as the world's greatest athlete.

Notes

Introduction: The Concept of an American Indian Hero

1. Glenn S. Warner, "The Indian Massacres," *Collier's*, October 17, 1931.

Chapter 1: The Outdoorsman

2. Black Hawk, *Autobiography*, quoted in Robert Reising, *Jim Thorpe: The Story of an American Indian*. Minneapolis: Dillon Press, 1974.

3. Gregory Richards, *Jim Thorpe: World's Greatest Athlete*. Chicago: Childrens Press, 1984.

4. Letter from Arthur Wakolee to Robert W. Wheeler, November 10, 1967, quoted in Robert W. Wheeler, *Jim Thorpe: World's Greatest Athlete*. Norman: University of Oklahoma Press, 1975.

5. From Jim Thorpe's personal scrapbook, quoted in Wheeler, *Jim Thorpe*.

6. From Jim Thorpe's personal scrapbook, quoted in Wheeler, *Jim Thorpe*.

7. From Jim Thorpe's personal scrapbook, quoted in Wheeler, *Jim Thorpe*.

8. Letter from Arthur Wakolee to Robert W. Wheeler, January 3, 1968, quoted in Wheeler, *Jim Thorpe*.

9. From Jim Thorpe's personal scrapbook, quoted in Wheeler, *Jim Thorpe*.

10. From an interview with Chief Garland Nevitt, by Robert W. Wheeler, July 14, 1967, Dearborn, Michigan, quoted in Wheeler, *Jim Thorpe*.

11. Jack Newcombe, *The Best of the Athletic Boys: The White Man's Impact on Jim Thorpe*. Garden City, NY: Doubleday, 1975.

12. Quoted in Newcombe, *The Best of the Athletic Boys*.

Chapter 2: The Rookie

13. Newcombe, *The Best of the Athletic Boys*.

14. From an interview with Verna Whistler, by Robert W. Wheeler, August 14, 1967, Carlisle, Pennsylvania, quoted in Wheeler, *Jim Thorpe*.

15. From an interview with Pete Calac, by Robert W.

Wheeler, July 27, 1967, Canton, Ohio, quoted in Wheeler, *Jim Thorpe*.

16. Richards, *Jim Thorpe*.

17. Warner, "The Indian Massacres."

18. Warner, "The Indian Massacres."

19. *The New York Times*, October 27, 1907, sports section.

20. Glenn S. Warner, "Red Menaces," *Collier's*, October 31, 1931.

21. Quoted in Wheeler, *Jim Thorpe*.

22. Quoted in Walter H. Lingo, "The Life Story of Jim Thorpe," *Athletic World*, July 1923.

Chapter 3: The Olympian

23. From Jim Thorpe's personal scrapbook, quoted in Wheeler, *Jim Thorpe*.

24. From Jim Thorpe's personal scrapbook, quoted in Wheeler, *Jim Thorpe*.

25. Quoted in Wheeler, *Jim Thorpe*.

26. Newcombe, *The Best of the Athletic Boys*.

27. Quoted in Newcombe, *The Best of the Athletic Boys*.

28. From an interview with Avery Brundage, by Robert W. Wheeler, July 12, 1967, Chicago, Illinois, quoted in Wheeler, *Jim Thorpe*.

29. Richards, *Jim Thorpe*.

30. From Jim Thorpe's personal scrapbook, quoted in Richards, *Jim Thorpe*.

31. Wheeler, *Jim Thorpe*.

32. From an interview with Ralph Craig, by Robert W. Wheeler, January 18, 1968, Waynesboro, Virginia, quoted in Wheeler, *Jim Thorpe*.

33. Ralph Craig interview, quoted in Wheeler, *Jim Thorpe*.

34. Quoted in Richards, *Jim Thorpe*.

Chapter 4: The Example

35. From an interview with Arthur Martin, by Robert W. Wheeler, August 15, 1967, Carlisle, Pennsylvania, quoted in Wheeler, *Jim Thorpe*.

36. From an interview with Joseph Alexander, by

Robert W. Wheeler, September 2, 1967, New York City, quoted in Wheeler, *Jim Thorpe*.

37. *The New York Times*, November 10, 1912, sports section.

38. From Jim Thorpe's personal scrapbook, quoted in Wheeler, *Jim Thorpe*.

39. From an interview with former president Dwight D. Eisenhower, by Robert W. Wheeler, August 17, 1967, Gettysburg, Pennsylvania, quoted in Wheeler, *Jim Thorpe*.

40. Quoted in Richards, *Jim Thorpe*.

41. From Jim Thorpe's personal scrapbook, quoted in Wheeler, *Jim Thorpe*.

42. From Jim Thorpe's personal scrapbook, quoted in Wheeler, *Jim Thorpe*.

43. From Jim Thorpe's personal scrapbook, quoted in Wheeler, *Jim Thorpe*.

44. From Jim Thorpe's personal scrapbook, quoted in Wheeler, *Jim Thorpe*.

45. Quoted in Reising, *Jim Thorpe*.

46. Quoted in Lawrence S. Ritter, *The Glory of Their Times: The Story of the Early Days of Baseball, Told by the Men Who Played It*. New York: Macmillan, 1966.

Chapter 5: The Professional

47. From Jim Thorpe's personal scrapbook, quoted in Wheeler, *Jim Thorpe*.

48. From an interview with Al Schacht, by Robert W. Wheeler, August 22, 1967, New York City, quoted in Wheeler, *Jim Thorpe*.

49. Quoted in Richards, *Jim Thorpe*.

50. From Jim Thorpe's personal scrapbook, quoted in Wheeler, *Jim Thorpe*.

51. Al Schacht interview, quoted in Wheeler, *Jim Thorpe*.

52. Al Schacht interview, quoted in Wheeler, *Jim Thorpe*.

53. Quoted in Richards, *Jim Thorpe*.

54. Quoted in Wheeler, *Jim Thorpe*.

Chapter 6: The Drifter

55. Art Cohn, *Long Beach Press-Telegram*, November 13, 1929.

56. Quoted in Richards, *Jim Thorpe*.

57. From an interview with Slim Harrison, by Robert W. Wheeler, July 20, 1967, San Pedro, California, quoted in Wheeler, *Jim Thorpe*.

58. Frank Scully and Norman Sper, "Jim Thorpe: The Greatest Athlete Alive," *American Mercury*, August 1943.

59. Quoted in Richards, *Jim Thorpe*.

60. Quoted in Wheeler, *Jim Thorpe*.

61. From an interview with Grace Thorpe, by Robert W. Wheeler, August 3, 1974, Washington, DC, quoted in Wheeler, *Jim Thorpe*.

62. From Jim Thorpe's personal scrapbook, quoted in Wheeler, *Jim Thorpe*.

63. From Jim Thorpe's personal scrapbook, quoted in Wheeler, *Jim Thorpe*.

Chapter 7: The Legend

64. From Jim Thorpe's personal scrapbook, quoted in Wheeler, *Jim Thorpe*.

65. From Jim Thorpe's personal scrapbook, quoted in Wheeler, *Jim Thorpe*.

66. From Jim Thorpe's personal scrapbook, quoted in Wheeler, *Jim Thorpe*.

67. Richards, *Jim Thorpe*.

68. From Jim Thorpe's personal scrapbook, quoted in Wheeler, *Jim Thorpe*.

69. *Los Angeles Mirror*, August 21, 1951.

70. From Jim Thorpe's personal scrapbook, quoted in Wheeler, *Jim Thorpe*.

71. Quoted in Richards, *Jim Thorpe*.

72. Quoted in Richards, *Jim Thorpe*.

73. *The New York Times*, March 29, 1953.

74. Quoted in Richards, *Jim Thorpe*.

75. Quoted in Richards, *Jim Thorpe*.

Epilogue: The World's Greatest Athlete

76. From an interview with Joe Boyle, by Robert W. Wheeler, August 20, 1967, Jim Thorpe, Pennsylvania, quoted in Wheeler, *Jim Thorpe*.

77. Joe Boyle interview, quoted in Wheeler, *Jim Thorpe*.

78. *New York Daily News*, October 13, 1973.

79. Richards, *Jim Thorpe*.

For Further Reading

William Heuman, *The Indians of Carlisle*. New York: G.P. Putnam's Sons, 1965. The story of the fabulous Indian track and football teams coached by Pop Warner in the first years of the twentieth century.

Robert Leckie, *The Story of Football*. New York: Random House, 1965. Well-written synopsis of the early days of the game, including several references to Thorpe and his contributions.

Don Nardo, *The Indian Wars*. San Diego: Lucent Books, 1991. An overview of the sad story of the destruction of Native American tribes by white American settlers and soldiers.

Robert Reising, *Jim Thorpe: The Story of an American Indian*. Minneapolis: Dillon Press, 1974. A good general synopsis of Thorpe's life.

Gregory Richards, *Jim Thorpe: World's Greatest Athlete*. Chicago: Childrens Press, 1984. Touches on the major events of Thorpe's life and athletic career. Includes many good quotes from newspaper articles, Thorpe's own scrapbook, and other works, but does not cite the sources of these quotes.

Gene Schoor, with Henry Gilfond, *The Jim Thorpe Story*. New York: Julian Messner, 1951. Good summary of Thorpe's life written before his death.

Robert Smith, *Illustrated History of Pro Football*. New York: Madison Square Press, 1970. Well-illustrated synopsis of the game.

Works Consulted

Wilbur J. Gobrecht, *Jim Thorpe, Carlisle Indian*. Carlisle, PA: Cumberland County Historical Society and Hamilton Library Association, 1972. Good general synopsis of Thorpe and his sports contributions.

Walter H. Lingo, "The Life Story of Jim Thorpe," *Athletic World*, July 1923. Overview of Thorpe's achievements up to that time, including some quotes about him by some who knew him.

Jack Newcombe, *The Best of the Athletic Boys: The White Man's Impact on Jim Thorpe*. Garden City, NY: Doubleday, 1975. Well-researched and clearly written study of Thorpe and his achievements, emphasizing his Indian heritage and how he and his fellow Carlisle players were affected by white culture.

Richard Henry Pratt, *Battlefield and Classroom: Four Decades with the American Indian, 1867-1904*. New Haven, CT: Yale University Press, 1964. Pratt recalls his experiences with the Indians, including his successful fight to establish the Carlisle Indian School.

Lawrence S. Ritter, *The Glory of Their Times: The Story of the Early Days of Baseball, Told by the Men Who Played It*. New York: Macmillan, 1966. A fact-filled volume of baseball lore.

John S. Steckbeck, *Fabulous Redmen. The Carlisle Indians and Their Famous Football Teams*. Harrisburg, PA: J. Horace McFarland, 1951. Well-written overview of Thorpe, Pop Warner, and the Carlisle athletes.

James E. Sullivan, ed., *The Olympic Games. Stockholm, 1912*. New York: American Sports Publishing Company, 1912. Overview of the events of the 1912 games, including Thorpe's original records.

Jim Thorpe, personal scrapbook (unpublished), inherited by his children, loaned to and extensively quoted from by Robert W. Wheeler in *Jim Thorpe: World's Greatest Athlete* (see below). Contains anecdotes about his childhood told in his own words, as well as comments by others, including clippings about his many sports triumphs.

Glenn S. Warner, "The Indian Massacres," *Collier's*, October 17, 1931; "Heap Big Run-Most-Fast," *Collier's*, October 24, 1931; "Red Menaces," *Collier's*, October 31, 1931. In these articles, coach Warner recalls many of the events involving Thorpe and other Indian players from the years when Carlisle was a top football and track school.

Robert W. Wheeler, *Jim Thorpe: World's Greatest Athlete*. Norman: University of Oklahoma Press, 1975. Excellent, detailed study of Thorpe's life, including many primary source quotes by Thorpe, Pop Warner, Thorpe's friends and relatives, and sportswriters. This is the primary source of material from Thorpe's personal scrapbook.

Index

Credits

Cover photo: Cumberland County Historical Society

AP/Wide World, 77, 81, 83

Archives & Manuscripts Division of the Oklahoma Historical Society, 13, 14 (bottom, left & right) 18, 35, 37, 60

The Bettmann Archive, 12, 14 (top), 46 (bottom), 62

Courtesy of the University of Illinois Archives, Avery Brundage Collection (1908-1975, R.S. 26/20/37, Box 311A, Scrapbook 18, p. 57), 42

Courtesy of the University of Illinois Archives, John R. Case Papers (1889-1984, R.S. 26/20/65, Box 2), 38

Culver Pictures, 19, 28, 49, 72, 76

Cumberland County Historical Society, 9, 10, 16, 21, 23, 24, 27 (both), 29, 31 (both), 32, 39, 40 (right), 41, 44, 45, 46 (top), 47, 52, 58, 75, 78, 79

Denver Public Library, Western History Department, 26 (both)

The Kansas State Historical Society, 20

UPI/Bettmann, 11, 40 (left), 57, 59, 64, 66, 67, 68, 70, 73, 74, 80, 85

Grateful acknowledgment is made to the University of Oklahoma Press for permission to reprint from *Jim Thorpe: World's Greatest Athlete*, by Robert W. Wheeler. Copyright © 1978 by the University of Oklahoma Press.

About the Author

Don Nardo is an actor, film director, and composer, as well as an award-winning writer. As an actor, he has appeared in more than fifty stage productions. He has also worked before or behind the camera in twenty films. Several of his musical compositions, including a young person's version of *The War of the Worlds* and an oratorio, *Richard III*, have been played by regional orchestras. Mr. Nardo has written short stories, articles, and more than forty-five books, including *Lasers, Gravity, Voodoo, Anxiety and Phobias, The Irish Potato Famine, Exercise, Democracy, The Mexican-American War, Charles Darwin, H.G. Wells, Ancient Greece,* and *The Extinction of the Dinosaurs.* Among his other writings are an episode of ABC's "Spenser: For Hire" and numerous screenplays. Mr. Nardo lives with his wife Christine on Cape Cod, Massachusetts.